DENYS JOHNSON-DAVIES

70 years translating contemporary Arabic literature

1922-2017

Photo by Paola Croci

I salute Denys Johnson-Davies as a dear friend, as an author, a reader and as an indomitable pioneering translator. His love of literature, his friendships with authors, with Banipal, and his long years in Cairo and Marrakech, marked him out as someone very special. The descriptions of him pile up – pioneer, doyen and dean of translators, excellent standard-bearer, unique figure, master artist, the great model for translators – his achievement is seminal, and we are all in massive debt to him, not least for the ease with which he moved between the living languages of Arabic and English. Many translators relate how influenced they have been by him – among their number leading literary translators today such as Roger Allen, William M Hutchins, Humphrey Davies and Khaled Mattawa.

A full tribute will be published in Banipal 60. Meanwhile, the second Saif Ghobash Banipal Prize Lecture on 7 November at the British Library in London will be an occasion for the two old friends Denys Johnson-Davies and Tayeb Salih to meet again in the words and thoughts of the lecturer Robert Irwin, whose topic is "*Season of Migration to the North*: The most important Arabic novel of the 20th Century".

Margaret Obank

Sheikh Hamad Award for Translation and International Understanding is accepting nominations for the year 2017 in the following categories:

1. Translation from Arabic into English (200,000 USD)
2. Translation from English into Arabic (200,000 USD)
3. Translation from Arabic into French (200,000 USD)
4. Translation from French into Arabic (200,000 USD)
5. Achievement Award (200,000 USD)

Sheikh Hamad Award for Translation and International Understanding is also accepting nominations for **achievement awards** in translation from and into the following Eastern languages:

Translation from Arabic into Chinese	(100,000 USD)
Translation from Chinese into Arabic	(100,000 USD)
Translation from Arabic into Japanese	(100,000 USD)
Translation from Japanese into Arabic	(100,000 USD)
Translation from Arabic into Malay	(100,000 USD)
Translation from Malay into Arabic	(100,000 USD)
Translation from Arabic into Persian	(100,000 USD)
Translation from Persian into Arabic	(100,000 USD)
Translation from Arabic into Urdu	(100,000 USD)
Translation from Urdu into Arabic	(100,000 USD)

Deadline for submissions is August 31/2017

Please visit our website **www.hta.qa/en**
for information about the Award, rules of submission and nomination forms.

HamadTAward

The Saif Ghobash Banipal Prize for Arabic Literary Translation Lecture

Robert Irwin on *Season of Migration to the North*: 'The most important Arabic novel of the 20th Century'

19.00-20.30
Tuesday 7 November 2017

The Knowledge Centre
British Library
96 Euston Road, London NW1 2DB

Tickets: £10 (£8 for Seniors, £7 other concessions)
To book, go to http://www.bl.uk/events

The masterpiece of the Sudanese writer Tayeb Salih (1929-2009), *Season of Migration to the North* was first published in Arabic in 1966 and in English translation by Denys Johnson-Davies in 1969.

It has been rightly subject to much analysis for treatment of colonialism, anti-colonialism, authoritarianism, resistance to social change and patriarchy. But this has been at the cost of more literary appraisals. The novel and its sequel *Bandarshah* drew upon the *Arabian Nights*, the Qur'an, pre-Islamic poetry and Sufi narratives, as well as *Heart of Darkness*, *Othello*, *The Tempest* and the writings of Freud. The stories Tayeb Salih told criticised those older narratives and they in turn commented on the stories he was telling.

In 2001 the Arab Literary Academy declared *Season of Migration to the North* to be 'the most important Arabic novel of the 20th century.' This is not a verdict that our speaker – the acclaimed writer on Arabic history and literature, Robert Irwin – intends to challenge.

Robert Irwin is a historian and writer of fiction and non-fiction. His non-fiction works include *The Arabian Nights: A Companion* (1994), *For Lust of Knowing: The Orientalists and Their Enemies* (2006), *Visions of the Jinn: Illustrators of the Arabian Nights* (2010) and *Memoirs of a Dervish* (2011) and in 2014 he edited and introduced *Tales of the Marvellous and News of the Strange* (a medieval Arab story collection). His seventh novel *Wonders Will Never Cease* was published in 2016, and his book on Ibn Khaldun is forthcoming in 2018.

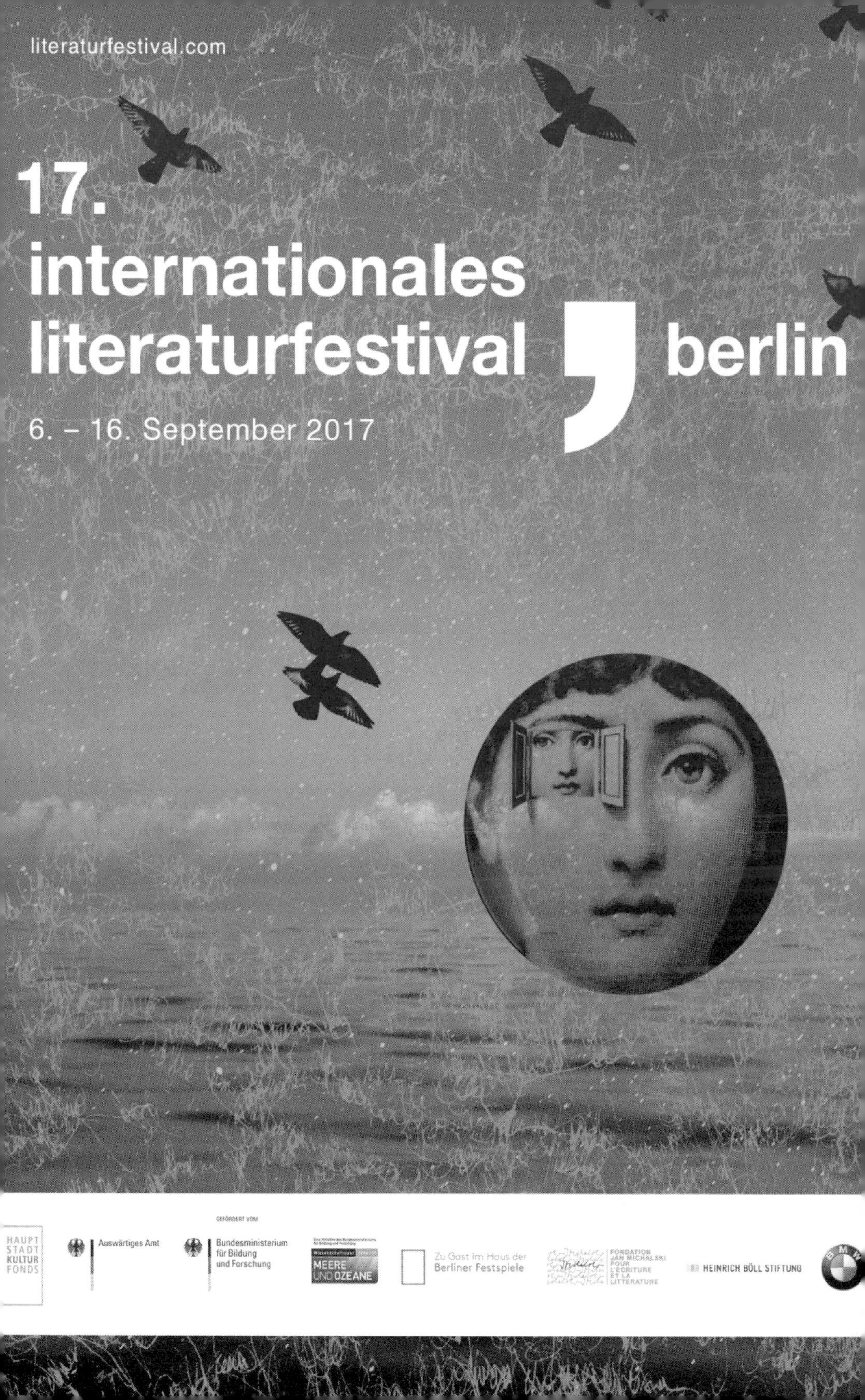

17. internationales literaturfestival berlin

6. – 16. September 2017

GEFÖRDERT VOM

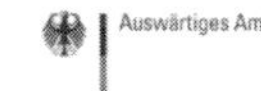

Bundesministerium
für Bildung
und Forschung

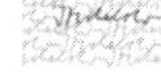

HEINRICH BÖLL STIFTUNG

DIGITAL BANIPAL

Complete archive now available for Institutions and individuals

Banipal's digital edition offers readers all over the world the chance to flip open the magazine on their computers, iPads, iPhones or android smartphones, wherever they are, check out the current issue, search through the back issues and sync as desired.

A digital subscription now gives full access to the complete digital archive, back to Banipal No 1, February 1998 – for individuals (£24.99) and for institutions (rate based on FTE). Print and digital subscriptions are still separate for the moment.

Download the free iTunes App or get it on an Android smartphone.

Preview the digital archive, preview the current issue or check out the Free Trial issue: *Banipal 53 – The Short Stories of Zakaria Tamer*

For more information, go to:
www.banipal.co.uk/subscribe/digital/

Trial issue

Subscribe Directly to Digital Banipal

Individual: exacteditions.com/banipal Libraries: institutions.exacteditions.com/banipal

Banipal's digital partner EXACT EDITIONS

BANIPAL
Magazine of Modern Arab Literature

WEBSITE: www.banipal.co.uk

EDITOR: editor@banipal.co.uk

PUBLISHER: margaret@banipal.co.uk

INQUIRIES: info@banipal.co.uk

SUBSCRIPTIONS: subscribe@banipal.co.uk

ADDRESS: 1 Gough Square, London EC4A 3DE

PRINTED BY Short Run Press Ltd
Bittern Road, Sowton Ind. Est. EXETER EX2 7LW

Photographs not accredited have been donated, photographers unknown.

This issue is ISBN 978-0-9956369-2-7. RRP £9, €12, USD15

BANIPAL, ISSN 1461-5363, is published three times a year by Banipal Publishing, 1 Gough Square, London EC4A 3DE

Banipal magazine, founded in 1998, takes its name from Ashurbanipal (668–627 BC), the last great king of Assyria and patron of the arts, whose outstanding achievement was to assemble in his capital Nineveh, Mesopotamia, from all over his empire, the first systematically organised library in the ancient Middle East. The thousands of clay tablets of Sumerian, Babylonian and Assyrian writings included the famous Mesopotamian epics of the Creation, the Flood, and Gilgamesh, many folk tales, fables, proverbs, prayers and omen texts.

Source: *Encyclopaedia Britannica*

www.banipal.co.uk

Habib Selmi

Renée Hayek

Ibrahim Farghali

Laila Al-Atrash

Sinan Antoon

Angel Guinda

Amir Tag Elsir

Yassin Adnan

Sultan al-Ameemi

Zuheir Al-Hiti

Abdelkarim Jouaiti

Viktoria Zarytovskaya

EDITORIAL

Summer Banipal is a chance to present a host of great reading opportunities, and our focus theme on The Longlist, featuring novels from the longlists of the International Prize for Arabic Fiction over the last two years, offers precisely that. In a number of previous issues we have published, in collaboration with the IPAF, dedicated features on the annual shortlists. One day we thought, let's give longlisted novels a chance to be showcased. Some authors have been longlisted more than once, while others have had works shortlisted, and some have translations, such as the 2013 longlisted novel *The President's Gardens* by Muhsin al-Ramli, which was published in English by Maclehose Press in April this year and has been wonderfully received and reviewed. We started off with a fairly long list, but have had to reduce it to eight novels for reasons of space.

Banipal 59 – The Longlist is packed with features, including for the first time a Guest Poet translated from Spanish – the great Angel Guinda who is recognised as "one of the most necessary and original poets in Spanish literature", and "an incorruptible voice". We are also proud to present, following features in earlier issues on Arabic literature in Japan and China, a fascinating essay by Russian Arabist Viktoria Zarytovskya on "Arabic Literature in Russia", from its first translations of the Qura'n to the lack of translators today.

We open the issue with chapters from the wonderfully descriptive and atmospheric ***Goat Mountain***, the debut novel 30 years ago of Tunisian author Habib Selmi, which Banipal Books will publish in 2018. It is a dark study of relationships and change when the newly appointed schoolteacher arrives at the isolated village of Goat Mountain after a long mule ride. Selmi has eight novels, with *The Scents of Marie Claire* (English 2010) shortlisted for IPAF in 2009, and *The Women of Al-Basatin* in 2012. Five of his novels are available in French translation, including *Goat Mountain*, and two in German.

We continue our successful **Literary Influences** series with Amir Tag Elsir, the Sudanese author, who tells us he became an avid reader at an early age due to his father loving books and pushing his sons to develop the same passion. One day, schoolboy Amir Tag Elsir composed a song that became a successful poem and that led to him writing his first novel when he graduated in medicine. To get it published he secretly pawned the Rolex watch his father had given him when he started university.

First up of the longlist novels is Moroccan author and journalist Yassin Adnan's debut novel ***Hot Maroc*** (both its Arabic and English title), a deliciously dramatic take on Marrakech's online world at the Atlas Lion Cubs cypercafé, where "the world becomes a small village", full of amazing dreams and ecstatic fantasies, via the fingertips of the customers of the café run by two competitive friends Rahal and Qamar.

The Temple of Silken Fingers by Egyptian author Ibrahim Farghali was longlisted for the 2016 IPAF and also won the 2017 Egyptian Sawiris Award. The book's narrator is a part-written manuscript abandoned by its author Rasheed, rescued by chance by a sailor, and which is determined to complete its blank pages as a memoir of Rasheed.

The opening chapter of Lebanese author Renée Hayek's novel ***The Year of the Radio***, the third of her novels to be longlisted for the IPAF (2009, 2011,

2017), sets the scene for the story of a young woman speech therapist living in modern-day Beirut. She is discharged from hospital after a horrific car crash and driven home by her parents – whom she doesn't get on with – and sets about wondering what on earth has happened to her life this last year, how after losing her job at a school for querying being used as a "surrogate teacher" all her plans "vanished in a puff of smoke". Readers will remain intrigued by the novel's title.

Days of Dust, by Zuhair al-Hiti, is the Iraqi author's third novel and first to be longlisted (2017). It follows the lives of a well-off Iraqi Muslim family living in the Bataween suburb of Baghdad after their old cook, Mary, a Christian, goes back to her natal village on the Nineveh plain to live out her last days. One of the family's daughters, Ghusn al-Ban, is captivated by the arrival of a new pastor for the Christian community, Father Fraidon, after bumping into him on the road, and starts to frequent his church in order to catch a glimpse or a whiff of his perfume and incense.

The Moroccans, by Abdelkarim Jouaiti, longlisted in 2017, is a family saga set in the central Moroccan town of Beni Mellal, in which the narrator, a schoolboy with deteriorating eyesight when we first meet him, is being looked after by his brother, a badly scarred and wounded ex-soldier. The novel unfolds the inseparable connections between local history, traditional customs, superstitions and modern technology in the boy fighting against going blind and in building workers discovering to their horror hundreds of human skulls as they dig the foundations of a new building.

One Room is Not Enough by Emirati author Sultan Al-Ameemi was longlisted for the 2017 IPAF, and revolves around an author, the protagonist, waking one morning in an unknown place to find the only thing he can do is spy on the life of an "Other", who seems to be an exact copy of himself, but then he must be spying on his own life. So, who is real, him or the Other? He abandons himself to this perplexing surreal adventure.

Hymns of Temptation by Palestinian novelist Laila Al-Atrash is her ninth novel, and the first longlisted (2016). Jerusalem's colourful and fraught history as the hub of the three monotheistic religions comes to life as film producer Rawia starts reading through forgotten papers of Father Haddad from the 1940s, discovering his "forbidden passion" for her elderly aunt, as well as a love story between a Greek monk and a Greek girl that had caused uproar in Jerusalem.

The final longlisted novel in our feature is ***Catalogue/Index*** by Sinan Antoon (longlisted 2017). This novel takes readers into the endless destruction and mayhem that characterises Iraq after 2003 through the relationship between an eccentric Baghdad bookseller, an Iraqi-American academic and translator (like the author himself) with family still in the city, and the pages of a catalogue/index that the former is obsessively compiling. He sends the translator a first part, "the history of the first minute of the war" which he hopes "will be a three-dimensional space" and through this somehow "change the past".

Happy holidays and Happy reading!!

Margaret Obank

1967

HABIB SELMI

GOAT MOUNTAIN

CHAPTERS FROM THE NOVEL

TRANSLATED BY CHARIS OLSZOK

Photo by: Ali Ghandtschi, Berlin

1

In all honesty, I was not as thrilled as I had expected to be. A slight tremor ran through me but nothing more. Then again, I have always been that way. I become feverishly engrossed, my entire being absorbed. But soon I lose interest and end up feeling hollow and empty. The truth is that I combine many such contradictions imperceptible to all but me: headstrong but ambivalent, level-headed but flighty. Do I deliberately conceal them? Perhaps. I have a capacity for dissimulation which sometimes takes even me by surprise. That day, I read my letter of appointment twice: first when I received it and later when I withdrew to the solitude of my room.

That evening, my brother played quietly and happily, and as my father performed the sunset prayer I felt sure that he was, for the first time, reciting the Fatiha at ease, relishing every word. The scent of grass drifted through the open windows, accompanied by the gentle croak of frogs and a trill in the distance, echoing like a woman's mournful wail. Goat Mountain. I do not deny that it was the name of the village itself that had intrigued me, and, without giving a thought to the actual place, a mammoth-like goat, with long, thick legs and a great udder swollen with milk enough to nourish the entire village, had materialised before my eyes. What other reason could there be for that name?

* * *

Bleached animal bones lay at the bottom of steep slopes. The bus was pungent with the scent of juniper and the wheels rumbled as it laboured up the sharp rises. Stretching out to east and west were endless expanses of tall dry grass and pine forests. In a fleeting dream, I saw myself sinking slowly but surely into coffee-coloured muddy soil.

My fellow passengers kept to themselves, seated as far from one another as possible. They had the mournful, reticent look of contagious invalids on their way to quarantine. Leaning to the left, I glimpsed the pallid features of my own face reflected in the spattered window pane.

After four hours, the bus pulled into a marketplace lined with wooden stalls. The driver switched off the engine.

"Al-'Ala!" the driver called, preparing to descend.

The passengers surged towards the door, and disappeared into the darkness while other men, who I later learned were merchants, surrounded the bus, electric torches in hands. Still others, barefoot and girded with leather belts, clambered on board and began unloading wares amidst the clamour and the cries.

The following morning, al-'Ala appeared larger than it had done the previous night. I was escorted by the bus driver to one of the shopkeepers who greeted me warmly and instructed me to follow him. We crossed the square at the far side of which stood a dusty tree, encircled by an iron railing. At the end of the row of stalls, we found ourselves surrounded by several houses with low doors. In a corner, a pair of goats stood tied to a metal ring and beside them mules were grazing on straw. I remained motionless, completely absorbed by the sight of the goats, one of which was endowed with a startlingly large udder. The shopkeeper, who had gone into one of the houses, emerged with a smile on his face.

"Stay here," he ordered me.

As I watched him disappear, I reflected on how lucky I was. My mother had said so too, weeping with joy at the news of my appointment. Later, after staunching her tears, she had reminisced about events from my childhood, grown hazy in my memory.

* * *

A voice drifted from the house, muffled as though it were coming from underground. The scent of moisture and damp straw hung in the air. As I walked towards the house, I had the distinct impression of approaching a holy shrine. Crossing the threshold, this impression increased as I found myself in a room, its floor covered with rush mats and its corners shrouded in darkness. A man was kneeling motionless on an old rug, a pitcher of water to his right. He was facing a wall on which hung a small lamp, its light reflected by the surrounding stone. I retreated but the man immediately rose to his feet and followed me out. I remember his smile clearly. It was a broad friendly smile but something about it disturbed me, though I was incapable of saying what. He saddled two mules and we set off. Having reached the far side of the marketplace, I turned to look back and saw the shopkeeper watching us leave. I waved to him and he waved back. To this day, I feel certain that he still remembers me.

After leaving the village, we mounted the mules, crossing through wide fields and trotting past shuttered houses and farmers herding their livestock. My companion stared straight ahead, thrusting his chin forward every now and then to indicate the direction. I glanced at his face, observing his wide dark eyes, ruddy lips and short hair, parted neatly down the middle with a precision that suggested an inordinate amount of care.

Having reached the top of a sandy rise, we began to descend the other side and I was forced to pull tightly on my reins and sit bolt upright for fear of falling from my mount. As I did so, the man turned to me.

"Be careful," he murmured, "The path's bumpy."

The sun rose in a crystal clear sky and my body began to trickle with sweat. During the first stretch of our journey, we occasionally glimpsed men on mules and donkeys, conversing with one another in raised voices that drifted to us from afar. Then, quite suddenly, we were confronted by nothingness. The ground stretched into the distance, bare but for several lone shrubs. The sound of the mules' hooves striking rhythmically on the ground rang clearly in my ears, lulling me to sleep. Although it was still morning, the heat was intense. As I raised my face to the sky, I felt as though we were the sole recipients of the sun's infernal blaze. Every particle of its heat seemed to be bearing down on us and us alone. My hands began to slacken and, every now and then, I was forced to release my grip on the reins so as to wipe drops of sweat from my eyes. Since receiving my letter of appointment, I had not once thought about what Goat Mountain might actually be like. How could this have escaped me? I gazed around at the silent, rosy landscape. For the first time I felt fear, tinged with regret, and heightened by the silence of the man leading me through that vast emptiness to an unknown destination. He remained taciturn, rigid on his mule as though fastened to it by leather straps.

We crossed a parched valley fringed by oleanders. The hooves of our mules sunk swiftly into the deep sand which bore no trace of man or animal, as though we were the first to set foot on its virgin surface. The man tugged on his reins, halting his mule by a carob tree which rose up incongruously in the arid landscape. I assumed that he intended to rest but he remained motionless, gazing at the tree as though seeing it for the first time. Then, without turning to me, he spoke:

"Here, seven men were slaughtered, their corpses left for the crows." He dismounted and began stirring the sand with his foot.

"Here they lie," he repeated, "Here they lie."

"Who slaughtered them?"

"The Pasha," he murmured, as though to himself.

He stood tense and unmoving, then, stretching out his hands and closing his eyes, several tears slid down his cheeks. As though sensing my discomfort, he brushed them brusquely away.

"My grandfather was among those men."

"Why were they killed?"

"For rebelling against the taxes," he replied after a short silence, speaking low as though divulging a secret.

He paused again, before embarking on a long speech, in which, with increasing relish, he described his grandfather, who had married three times and begotten eighteen sons. Five of them had travelled to the city and lost all contact with home. Others had died in tribal wars.

At first, his speech captivated me and I began to picture the corpses disintegrating beneath the blazing sun. Then, quite at random, I felt a wave of hatred rise within me, prompted by his tears. As I watched him, his face began to change, his features blurring into those of my father. This was a man about whom I knew nothing, except that he was the grandson of a rebel slaughtered in this obscure, mysterious terrain.

As we progressed steadily up a steep rise, the rocks around us multiplied and the path became too narrow for the mules to walk side by side. We moved forward in single file. Then, wending our way down the other side, we reached a small stream. Without a word, we pulled our mules simultaneously to a halt and dismounted. The man seated himself on the bank while I plunged my head into the water before scooping it up and splashing it onto my chest. I finally decided to immerse myself entirely, sinking happily under. Watching me, the man laughed.

"And what will you do in Goat Mountain?" he asked.

His question troubled me, perhaps because he had not asked it right from the first. I stopped splashing and, for a moment, considered not replying. Then, looking him squarely in the eyes, I answered.

"I will teach the children."

Without a word, he looked away then rose to his feet and mounted his mule.

His voice dripped sarcasm when he said as we set off once again: "So now they're worried about the children . . ."

2

Goat Mountain was not a large village. In the afternoons, dust started to swirl, dying down only at nightfall when the bats began their tireless circling. The school consisted of a single classroom which could hold up to thirty children. In its courtyard stood a mulberry tree which the residents of Goat Mountain estimated to be around three hundred years old, although they did not know who had planted it originally.

We arrived shortly after midday, passing by houses where naked children peeped through doorways. A crowd of men came to walk alongside us, peering intently up at me as though I had descended from some alien planet. In front of a small house, built on a slight rise at the far end of the village, my companion halted his mule and we dismounted. One of the men led the mules off to be watered and fed. I hovered, unsure what to do next, stripped of volition before the sea of enquiring eyes fixed upon me.

"This is the school," the man said, gesturing towards the building.

On hearing this, the men began muttering knowingly to one another and some of them broke into broad smiles before, eventually, heading off on their separate ways. I am certain that for many years these fathers will continue to talk of me as they harvest their potatoes, disagreeing, as the conversation stretches on, even as to the very appearance of the mule that I rode that day.

I spent the first night with my companion whose name, I learned, was Ismail. Even as I walked through the door, I was struck by the cleanliness of his house, boldly defying the sand storms which visited the village every afternoon without fail. The furniture was arranged with painstaking precision, but what truly astonished me was the tall wooden bookcase that was lined with large leatherbound volumes. Without asking permission, I headed straight to it, unable to rein in my curiosity, and began flicking through the tomes of Qur'anic exegesis, history, Islamic law and literature. Ismail turned to me, his lips curved into a smile.

"Those belonged to my grandfather."

I continued leafing through them.

"He was a great scholar," he said, adding: "He studied at the Zaytuna University for two years but had to leave early because his father couldn't afford the fees."

The next morning we went to the school. Ismail headed straight to the back of the classroom, weaving his way through the scattered wooden chairs towards a low door that I had overlooked on my first visit.

"This is your new home," he announced, opening the door, "If you need anything, please inform me. I am the government's representative in Goat Mountain." Astonished by his words, I stood motionless and suddenly the image of him standing beneath the carob tree, weeping for a grandfather long dead, flashed through my mind.

My home was made ready in a single day; the spiders' webs obliterated, the walls painted and the door and windows polished. Years later, as I watched the noontide light filtering through the small window of my cell, I recalled the first moments of my life in that house.

* * *

I spent the first days alone, keeping to myself. At nightfall, I would light my lantern and compose long letters to my family, telling them how the residents of Goat Mountain grew exceptional potatoes, how their children were intelligent and how terribly alone I felt. Their letters always took a long time to reach me. I would wait expectantly for the day when Ismail went to collect them from al-'Ala, the last delivery point. Within a short space of time, we grew very close. He introduced me to every family in the village, taking me round from house to house. But, in spite of that, I remained wary of him. Whenever we passed the mulberry tree, he would assure me that it was his grandfather who had planted it. He had bought the seedling in the city, Ismail told me, and, as it grew, he had built protective fencing around it to guard it from the cows and goats. It was he who had pruned it back every year and this, Ismail asserted, entitled him to exclusive rights over its fruits.

The isolation which he occasionally imposed on himself also intrigued me. For days on end he would remain in his house, talking to no one. In order to save money so as to accomplish his grandfather's dying wish, he often consumed only boiled potatoes, larks caught in snares or wild plants uprooted from the vegetation surrounding his house. On other occasions, however, he would embark on a lavish shopping spree in al-'Ala, returning laden with shoes, socks, trousers and saddlebags stuffed with tins of his beloved sardines, as well as vials of perfume which he lined up on the bookcase. The inhabitants of Goat Mountain observed him with ironic smiles.

"He'll meet the same end as his grandfather," they murmured to one another.

At the beginning of every month, Ismail went from house to house, noting down all new births, a pair of steel-rimmed spectacles inherited from his grandfather perched on his nose. With utmost care, he recorded the names of the babies, their fathers, mothers, grandfathers and grandmothers in an imposing logbook and, on Thursdays, he copied them into the official government files in al-'Ala. He would often grow agitated when the new parents could not specify the exact time of birth and sometimes he would even remove the coverlet from the baby and flip it over to confirm its sex. The inhabitants of Goat Mountain, he informed me, only thought of such matters when their babies had already begun to crawl around. At the end of every month, meanwhile, Ismail would gather everyone beneath the mulberry tree and read to them from a newspaper that was always a week out of date. After reviewing everything of import, he would tell his audience that the soil of Goat Mountain was fertile, that it produced the world's finest potatoes and that the government would soon add new rooms to the school, build a hospital, and lay a wide road through the mountains, connecting Goat Mountain to al-'Ala. They would tarmac the dirt roads and exterminate the insects and rodents, and Goat Mountain would be transformed into a great city frequented by ministers, and it will attract the lottery, circuses, famous bands, and tourists coming to see their exceptional potato farming. Ismail would begin his monologue softly but his voice grew gradually louder as he progressed, his eyes glowing and spittle flying from his mouth.

* * *

Then one day everything changed. I often try to reconstruct the exact details of the scene in my head. At first, it remains hazy but I pursue it stubbornly until I can almost inhale the scent of the wooden chairs. I was standing in the classroom, facing the blackboard. Moving my head slightly, I caught sight of Ismail. He moved through the chairs to the back of the class and took a seat. That night I found him at home, totally absorbed in writing while soaking his lower legs in a bucket of water. Seeing me hovering in the doorway, he lifted his head. Fatigue was writ plainly across his features. He gave a forced smile then looked down again.

"I'm writing a report about you," he said, "about your teaching."

He shifted his legs about in the bucket and gave another smile. I stood rooted to the spot, feeling a cold shiver down my spine. Saying nothing, I went to gaze intently at the rainbow of colours cast by his oil lamp. Ismail seemed to relax, leaning back against the wooden chair.

"You understand . . . don't you?" he asked, putting his pen down, "It's my job."

He fell silent for a moment and then continued, toying with the pen.

"I cannot remain silent . . ."

"About what?" I interrupted him.

He sprang instantly to his feet.

"Don't think me so gullible," he roared, "I know your tricks."

He fell silent. I saw his right hand slacken. He sat back on the chair, looking at me as though he would like to continue speaking.

The next time he came to the school, I stood blocking the doorway. I was furious and had determined to confront him. He did not attempt to push past me but simply grinned broadly and turned on his heel, walking slowly away and glancing to left and right. I continued watching him until he had crossed the courtyard. As he disappeared, I felt as though I had won a victory and the idea that Ismail was my enemy became embedded in my mind.

Several days later I discovered that he was no longer talking to me. My letters began to arrive later and later. I would receive only one a month and then they stopped altogether, completing my isolation.

It is not easy to live alone in a small village like Goat Mountain. I awoke to this reality after my first burst of enthusiasm. I buried myself in study but could not dispel my loneliness. One night I decided not to light my lantern and remained in darkness. Anger seized me and I tossed and turned feverishly on my mattress, sinking into a long spell of delirium. I had read and reread all the books I had brought with me and they no longer offered any respite or consolation. Sometimes, I would spend hours tending to my hair, combing it to the right before ruffling it up and brushing it back to the left. Otherwise, I would clip my nails or stand in front of the mirror examining the colour of my eyes and trying to decide whether they were blue or green or yellowish green or bluish yellow. I developed strange new pastimes: counting all of my notebooks with black covers and then all those with red ones; measuring the length and breadth of my bedroom; taking my razor apart and putting it together again; or simply gazing at my hands and trying to determine which was larger. When my depression grew particularly severe I would take out my letter of appointment, contemplate it then fold it back up and return it to its place.

During that same period, Ismail went into one of his periods of retreat. He would wake early and go for a short, lonely walk through the fields adjoining his house before disappearing inside once again. His absence allowed me to become better acquainted with the people of Goat Mountain. I began visiting them regularly, playing with their children and occasionally accompanying them to the fields to help dig potatoes. Little by little I overcame my loneliness and no longer worried so much about not receiving letters. I felt sure that all was well at home. I began to love Goat Mountain and soon felt as though I had been born in one of its small dwellings. The village became the centre of my universe.

3

The people of Goat Mountain grow outstanding potatoes. Digging their fingers into the freshly ploughed earth, they carefully press in each tuber and with quick, deft movements cover them with earth. I can no longer remember why I found it so strange. It is true that I have never liked potatoes and during my stay in Goat Mountain (was it three years or four?) I did not eat a single one. Their colour, however, has always intrigued me.

Many stories are told in Goat Mountain about potatoes. I listened to them intently and at night, when I was alone, would write them down in a small notebook which I have kept with me ever since. At first, I compared the different tales, attempting to ascertain which was most authentic. Gradually, however, I gave this up and began to love them all. They seemed to be, at the same time, both real and fanciful. When I recall them now, I allow myself to alter them slightly, embellishing them with details of my own. To a story told by an attractive widow in her fifties, known by three names – Khadija, Bint Burawi and al-Burawiyya – I added a new beginning:

"One morning, not far from Ismail's house, we came across a new plant, ripe and green as though it had just poked through the earth. It was the children who noticed it. Pulling it from the earth, they discovered that it was not a weed as they had at first thought. They took it back to their parents who examined it closely. Several of them chewed a bit to try its flavour. After much discussion, they agreed that it was most likely a strange strain of colocynth with no nutritional value, especially given that neither the cattle nor the chickens would eat it and even the roosters kept their distance. They discarded the plant and its small tubers, which reminded them of partridge eggs. After some time, however, the plant reappeared. It was again the children who discovered it. A large number of the plants had spread over the ground. They gathered up the tubers, took them home and, after cooking them, discovered them to be delicious. Thus began potato fever in Goat Mountain."

I do not like the beginning of the second story and always omit it. The old man who narrated it clearly lacked imagination.

"My grandfather," he related, "was the first resident of Goat Mountain to visit the city. While there, he witnessed many remarkable things that he continued to recount to the end of his days. It was there that he discovered certain small vegetables, which he ate with great delight. I remember him returning with a bag full of potatoes and being quite incapable of defining their colour. God bless my grandfather. Without him, Goat Mountain would have remained in poverty."

I was told the story of the soldier on three separate occasions and can no longer remember who I heard it from first. Forgetting the original author, however, granted my imagination free rein and I always experience immense joy when I replay it in my mind: "One autumn evening (the story does not specify the season so I have added this small detail), a tall, green-eyed soldier arrived mysteriously in the village. He rode a beautiful chestnut horse whose snorts and whinnies filled the streets. The soldier lived in Goat Mountain for twenty years during which he taught its people to grow potatoes, led them to victory in thirteen tribal wars, built a house at the end of the village and married a woman ten years his junior who died four months after marrying him. None of the residents of Goat Mountain knew the woman's family for they lived in a distant village." As for the house that the soldier built, according to the story it still stands at the end of the village. When my conflict with Ismail grew particularly bad, I left the school and took up residence there.

* * *

Dust. Barking dogs. The aroma of cooking food. Mules plodding and chickens strutting. The day of the potato market is no ordinary day in Goat Mountain for, in a village where weddings are few and far between, the people seize every opportunity for a celebration. The freshly dug potatoes are loaded into goatskin sacks or simply piled high in front of houses. At noon, the merchants arrive from al-'Ala.

Ismail did not live off potato farming like the other villagers despite having inherited a substantial parcel of land from his grandfather. He prided himself on being a government employee and collecting a large salary on the first Thursday of every month. Certain years, however, he would develop a strange interest in his land, entrusting its cultivation to one of the village men. Thus, it was potatoes that would end his solitude, propelling him back into the company of the people of Goat Mountain.

One day, Ismail, in his usual brusque manner, announced that he would soon journey to Mecca for Hajj. He went back and forth from al-'Ala, preparing for his departure, then shut himself away in his house for two full days. His forthcoming pilgrimage remained the main topic of conversation in the village for quite some time. Although the people of Goat Mountain regarded many of his claims with a certain degree of scepticism, they were proud that someone from their small, forgotten village would set foot on holy ground. That season, the harvest was abundant and the earth yielded more potatoes than ever before. Having filled every sack and storehouse, piles of potatoes remained dotted across the fields. The children played games with them and fed them to the animals until they could manage no more. After giving thanks to God, the villagers began to ponder the cause of such abundance. Given that the ground was the same as always and that the rainfall had been as usual, each one could not help but secretly think of Ismail's Hajj.

A great surprise awaited them, however – one that the villagers had never imagined possible. A month went by and the merchants of al-'Ala did not appear. Eventually, Ismail gathered everyone under the mulberry tree and told them that the potato harvest had been abundant everywhere that year, and farmers had ended up throwing their excess crops into the sea. After a long silence, he added in a low voice, looking each one of them in the eye:

"I have decided to buy every potato in Goat Mountain."

Shouts of joy arose, accompanied by boisterous applause. Several of the men began to dance. Ismail, meanwhile, simply reminded everyone that he was the grandson of a revolutionary who had died defending their ancestors.

4

That afternoon, the heat was intense and the silence oppressive. I closed the windows and door and threw myself onto my mattress. I was tired and anxious. I tried to sleep but could not and so allowed my thoughts to wander freely and at random, a trick which I often resort to. Attempting to forget my surroundings, I retreat into the past in search of a distant image: chasing away cows quenching their thirst at a well, fighting with other children over a dead lark, or trying to forge a swollen river. Tossing and turning on the mattress, I heard the squeak of the door behind me and turned instantly around. Ismail stood on the threshold. I leapt to my feet.

"Welcome," I cried mechanically.

Ismail continued to watch me and I felt a great wave of uneasiness washing over me. I invited him in, indicating the only chair in the room.

"Sit down. Please."

He went to the chair, sweeping his gaze across the room as though searching for something. We remained in silence. Ismail stretched out his legs, revealing his sandals. I gazed fixedly at his feet and toes until he drew his legs back beneath the chair.

"It's extremely hot," I said.

He nodded in agreement and we fell silent again. I sat on the edge of the bed, wondering why he had suddenly decided to visit. He had not spoken to me since the incident at the school and had gone out of his way to isolate me and push me into leaving. Immersed in these thoughts, I heard him speak.

"Have you heard the news?"

Although eager to learn why he had come, his question alarmed me for some reason. Perhaps it was because I felt that he was waiting for me to burst out eagerly: "What news?" I lifted my head and gazed at the ceiling, reckoning that my silence might humiliate him. He shifted on his chair and I turned to find his unwavering gaze upon me. I stared back at him for several seconds and then, ill at ease, lowered my head and clasped my hands together. When I looked up again, I discovered that he was still watching me, a half smile hovering on his lips. I smiled back.

"What's up?" I asked mechanically.

NEXT ISSUE

Chapter from

The Kitsch 2011

A novel by Tunisian writer and journalist

Safi Said

Translated by Jonathan Wright

"Have you heard the news?" he repeated, stretching his neck from side to side.

"What's happened?"

"War's broken out between the Jews and the Arabs."

"When?" I asked, leaning slightly towards him.

"I heard about it yesterday."

He fell silent and lowered his head. I recalled the neat parting, which had once divided his hair, and wondered whether he was now trying to cover up the onset of baldness with a new style. He raised his head.

"The Arabs are demanding a ceasefire."

"The Arabs are demanding a ceasefire," I repeated with an indifference that took even me by surprise. "But why?" I added, after a pause.

I believe that my question displeased him, that it pained him somewhat to hear it. He leaned to the left and gazed up at the ceiling. I took two steps towards him, trying to think of something to say. He stood up in turn and moved towards the door.

"But that's not why I came," he said, without looking at me.

"Then why did you come," I asked after a slight hesitation.

He turned to me, putting his hands in his pockets.

"I have some letters for you."

As I went to take them, he spoke again, in a quite different tone.

"On one condition."

In a flash, I realised that he had come to torment me and that everything he had said thus far was simply a preamble for this condition. I considered rushing at him headlong and snatching the letters from his hands but managed to hold myself back.

"What is it?" I asked, backing off.

He followed me, his face mere inches from mine.

"Stop provoking the villagers against me," he said, his wide eyes fixed on me.

"I haven't provoked anyone against you," I cried, seized by a sudden rage.

"Yes, you have!" he yelled, and I felt his spit on my face. He fell silent for a moment. "I know your tricks," he added, his eyes on mine, "You've spread rumours that I'm working with the merchants from al-'Ala."

"They're not stupid, even the children know," I said quietly, trying

Jabal al-Anz (Goat Mountain)

to appease him. "And those letters which you want to give me are of no importance to me," I added, returning to the bed.

"Are you sure about that?"

"Yes," I replied firmly, but knew as soon as I saw his smiling face that I had not convinced him. "You can keep them," I said with complete conviction. "Take them. I know how much you love letters," I added scornfully after a moment's hesitation.

I had hoped that my words would madden him and longed to see him enraged, but he simply smiled again and sat back down on the chair.

I stationed myself in turn on the edge of the bed, clasping my hands together and watching him as he rubbed his face. Several minutes went by and I could tell that Ismail was thinking neither of my letters nor of the inhabitants of Goat Mountain, nor of the war between the Arabs and the Jews. He shuffled his feet and inclined his head slightly.

"Do you remember our journey to Goat Mountain?"

He was changing the topic, seeking refuge in the past as I so often did. I was briefly struck by the impression that, deep down, we were one and the same. But, at the same time, I sensed that his question had other, hidden, motives. What did he want?

I plumped the pillow and leaned nonchalantly against it.

"Yes . . . I remember."

He slumped into his chair, stretching his legs. "You may not believe what I am about to tell you but that doesn't matter to me. I was so happy when I first saw you. From that moment, I felt as though your arrival in Goat Mountain would transform my life. This feeling only increased when you took an interest in my grandfather's library and started flicking through his books. You're the first person who's ever done that . . . If you only knew the life I lead in this remote village . . ." He fell silent, as though waiting for a signal to continue. I could tell he had a pressing need to talk, and gave a nod of my head, indicating that I was not annoyed. This seemed to comfort him.

"My life here has been tough. Sometimes, I shut my doors and windows just so I don't have to see anyone. I used to love reading, especially epics and histories. But that soon turned to repulsion and I have never understood why. I began to hate books. Their very shape and smell disgusted me. One night I dreamt that I was climbing a staircase of books and that I fell from the top onto a ground covered in icy water. You were the only person who could rescue me. I was convinced of that. I needed someone to help me but you let me down, just like everyone else."

"I let you down?" I interrupted in astonishment.

"Maybe you didn't do so on purpose but you did let me down. When you found out I was writing a report on you, you were angry with me without even trying to understand why I was doing it. I had to write it. What else can I do in this remote village other than write reports?"

I sat up straight and gazed at him in bewilderment. He rubbed his hands together and stood up, looking towards the door. "I must tell you that I am stubborn," he said. "My grandfather was too," he added, as though to himself. I left the bed and went over to him.

"But I don't understand. What . . ."

"I don't care about anything any more," he interrupted, turning towards me. Then, taking the letters from his pockets, he threw them to the floor and left.

Jabal al-Anz (Goat Mountain) is the first novel of Tunisian writer Habib Selmi. It was published by al-Mu'assasa al-Arabiya Lil-Dirassat wal-Nashr, Beirut, 1988. *Goat Mountain*, translated by Charis Olszok, will be published by Banipal Books in Spring 2018

Literary Influences

Banipal regularly invites a prominent Arab author to write about the books and authors that have had an influential impact on their life and work.

Sudanese author Amir Tag Elsir was shortlisted for the IPAF in 2011, longlisted twice in 2014 and 2017, and in 2015 was one of the winners of the Katara Prize. He has published 16 novels, with a growing number translated, 3 biographies and 3 poetry collections. Here he recounts his illuminating adventure with reading and writing.

AMIR TAG ELSIR

"I pawned my Rolex to publish my first book"

First and foremost, I was a reader. Before trying to write even a single letter, my brothers and I were all readers. I think our generation all had a similar experience in this. Beside the poets and writers that emerged, even those who never entered the fray of writing themselves have nevertheless at least remained devoted and loyal to reading. It's rare to find someone from my generation who doesn't read and comment on books.

In the 1970s, we were living in Port Sudan on the coast of the Red Sea, where my father Tag Elsir Mohammed Nour worked in customs at the port. Despite his official duties and limited opportunities, he was an active reader of all kinds of material. He had a large library and took every chance he could to fill it with books and spend hours sitting and reading, especially on Fridays and in the evenings when there were no guests to interrupt his contemplation. Among the books in that library, I remember the complete works of Mahmoud al-Aqqad, Taha Hussein's *The Days*, Tawfiq al-Hakim's books and those of Colin Wilson, the Arabic epic *Taghribat Bani Hilal*, some poetry collections of Al-Mutanabbi, Al-Farazdaq, Imru' al-Qais, and I remember from modern poetry Abdel Rahman el-Abnudi and others. We were four brothers at the time and, although we were only in primary school, we could read children's books and had to go and discuss them with our father.

Port Sudan

Mr Tag Elsir Mohammed Nour laid down his own special law, following the siren song of knowledge. The law stated that every week a suitable book would be brought to the house for us, which we would all read before another arrived the following week. He had an agreement with a bookshop owner he knew, called Rifat Dhiraar, to deliver the books. He would come on Mondays, as I recall, at an appointed time in the afternoon, riding a motorbike, whose sound we recognised. He wouldn't knock on the door, but would throw the book over the wall, where we would all be waiting to fight over it, each wanting to be the first to read it.

At first it really was a law that we had to follow; we might even be punished or have our pocket money docked if we fell behind in our reading. With time, however, it was less of a rule and became more a part of the fabric of our individual personalities. The thrilling visits of Rifat, with his special children's books and magazines, came to an end. But the same thirst for knowledge has remained ever since. At that time, we also discovered a very important teacher and teller of stories called Hamza. He was a very old man living with some of his relatives in one of the neighbourhood houses. He was a simple trader with a wooden cart outside the gates of the hospital, but every Friday evening he would gather as many of the neighbourhood children as he could in the courtyard of the house where he lived and read them wonderful stories from the books he owned and kept hidden under his bed. These only increased our appetite for reading. I remember the tales of Cinderella and Sindbad and many others that had some wisdom or moral to impart. In the years after that extraordinary reader-teacher died, when I was becoming more independent and was able to roam the market with a special allowance from my father, I became acquainted with all the book stores in the city: Okasha's, Atta al-Manan's, Al-Nahda, Al-Amudi's. They were all filled with contemporary books, trying to amass

"Adventures of Sindbad" front cover

Taha Hussein

Somerset Maugham

everything coming out of Cairo, Beirut and anywhere else that was publishing. Mr Okasha owned a small book shop near my home, in front of the municipal park, and was the one who showed the most interest in my intellectual cravings; he would loan me books in exchange for a negligible fee, thereby allowing me to become familiar with most of what was being published at that time: everything by Al-Aqqad and Taha Hussein, Yahya Haqqi and Tawfiq al-Hakim, W. Somerset Maugham, Albert Camus, and hundreds more. This was in addition to poets like Ahmed Abdel Muti Hijazi, Salah Abdel Sabour, Badr Shakir al-Sayyab, Abdul Wahab al-Bayati, Amal Donqol and others. I had my own rule to read a book every three days, and kept that up until I was at university. Then life and its pressures, especially the burdens of family and work, as well as creative writing, started eating into more of my time. I was reading with the same passion but without the old routine. You'd often find me in some predicament, going over the many new writers I wanted to read and offer an opinion on, but not able to find the time to do so.

Inspiration for creative writing came to me suddenly. Perhaps it wasn't so sudden, but it took me a while to realise it was there. I've never forgotten that autumn day in Al-Abyad (White City), in western Sudan. We had moved there for my father's work, which could take him, as an employee of the state, from one town to another at a moment's notice. It was a gorgeous city and really flourished in the autumn; you could smell the sweet scent of rain even if it wasn't the wet season. I was in middle school at the time and I was riding my bike through the streets of El-Qubbah, where we lived, which was one of the central districts. There was a huge dome there where Sheikh Ismail al-Wali was buried; he was a well-known authority on

Amal Donqol

Badr Shakir al-Sayyab

Sufism and his style of leadership is still followed by his descendants to this day. I started singing a song that was popular at the time, but then I forgot some of the words, so filled in the blanks with some phrases of my own. I kept singing, with my own bits, following the melody of the song whose words I'd forgotten, until I finished it in my mind as a complete poem. I felt intoxicated. I changed direction and returned home to take out a notebook I'd bought but not yet used. I wrote down the poem as it was in my head, then added to it and made it a finished piece complete with feeling and melancholy. My exhilaration soared. Early the next morning, I took it to my father's secretary, her name was Nagat, to type up ten copies for me. I distributed these to the teachers at school and reaped a lot of praise. A few days later, one of my classmates told me that his uncle, a famous singer in the city, liked the song and would set it to music and perform it. That was the pinnacle of my excitement! When the song rang out through the city at night, no one could believe that the words were by a school boy.

We stayed in Al-Abyad for two years, during which time I wrote dozens of songs to the point that composition became a very normal thing for me. When we returned to Port Sudan and I started high school, my world expanded to include poets, singers, dramatists and writers. I would meet them on Thursday evenings at the Writers' and Artists' Union. There were many songs in circulation in Port Sudan's night scene. I went myself to public and private concerts where I knew the organisers and would recite my poems confidently, without any apprehension. These encounters were fruitful and beneficial.

I then travelled to Egypt to study medicine. I can say that this was the most fertile period for me in terms of discovering more influ-

"Studying medicine in Cairo"

ences which broadened my own experience and positioned me in the ranks of modernist poets. I forged rich relationships with books that hadn't been available to me in Sudan, and made friends with writers and poets who were stars, some of whom are still going. During that period, after studious reading of both poetry and criticism, following the cultural journals that were being published, I was able to write modern poetry in free verse, which was the most beautiful and animated style of the time and still has a wide audience today. I wrote dozens of poems, drawing inspiration from the crises of my country and my personal life, a little on politics, a little on love, a lot from society. By the last year of my studies, my poetry was famous and was being published by the biggest newspapers and magazines in the Arab world, including *Ebda'*, *Al-Kahera*, and *Asharq al-Awsat* and *Majalla* which are published in London, as well as others. But then suddenly I gave up poetry.

It was at the end of 1977, I had finished my studies in medicine and was ready to return to my country, when I felt that I had it in me to write a novel. I spent a whole month writing by night and sleeping by day. The result was that I produced a short text, a mix of poetry and prose. My elation with that text was on a par with how I felt when I wrote my first poem on that day in Al-Abyad.

That poetic novel was called *Karmakul*, after the village where I was born in North Sudan. Trying to get it published was exhausting. Although the Egyptian writers that I knew from the cafés read and enjoyed samples from it, the few publishing houses at that time firmly refused to look at it. Whenever I went and presented my book, the manager would say: "We only publish established authors." Naturally it was disappointing but I didn't give up. I had a token of wealth around my wrist in the form of a gold Rolex that my father had given me when I started university. I pawned it very easily and took the money to pay a small publisher called Al-Ghad (Tomorrow), owned by the late poet Kamal Abdul Haleem, to publish my book. I distributed it myself among students, carrying copies in a shoulder bag from city to city until I had earned enough to buy back my watch. I would need it years later for another important job; when I was first away in Doha, I had to sell it in order to live until I received my first pay cheque.

I worked for years in Sudan, where I gathered many stories, tales and even legends, but I stopped writing completely. I was swept up by my work. It gave me an understanding of people, of authentic characters, and the things I saw and heard in the sick wards, in the houses I visited – especially in the villages where I worked as a medical examiner – and in the clinic I founded on the outskirts of Port Sudan. No one knows the secrets of those slums except those who have delved in and uncovered them. I think doctors do more of this excavating than most, since it is they who carry people's most intimate secrets.

To date I have published sixteen novels, three biographies, and other books of short pieces and poetry. I can say that my writing experience is built on a celebration of imagination and trying to create an atypical style; it may be influenced by older works but has its own particular form and flavour. Ever since I started, I've used poetic imagery and mythical characters. Even when I'm writing a contemporary novel about a real city and a real situation, the rhythm of a fable runs through the writing, so of course there are strange words and actions. This is a style that I like personally. In the beginning, I may have been influenced by Latin American writers, their magic and use of extreme imagination. I'm thinking especially of Gabriel Garcia Marquez, whom I consider one of my early teachers. I first came across his novels while I was studying in Egypt and then read everything he had written, many times. I was overwhelmingly inspired by *Love in the Time of Cholera*. The important thing is that I found my way. I was interested in thorny human issues, and I made use of my imagination, which I had consistently honed and nurtured. The novels I write are inspired by history but do not depict real history. I borrow details from a given period to use them as a backdrop for a text that could be set in any epoch. I don't like documentary style writing; I don't think it allows enough artistic freedom. It restricts the writer to real events, which can never be developed according to his imagination; and if he were to alter them, they may end up doing a disservice to particular characters that have a different existence in memory from the one he wants to fashion for them. I wrote an epic novel called *The Yelling Dowry*, which is about the fantastical Sultanate of Ansaaba (an allegory for the old Sultanate of Darfur), in the time of a particular Sultan. It was a way of talking about current events in the context of something old, a way of safely explaining instruments of oppression. A young man loses his masculinity for the sake of a dream, his sister dies of a broken heart, and he lives trapped under tyranny. I wanted it to be a reading of reality and I think it has a profound and disruptive impact on the minds of those that read it. I also

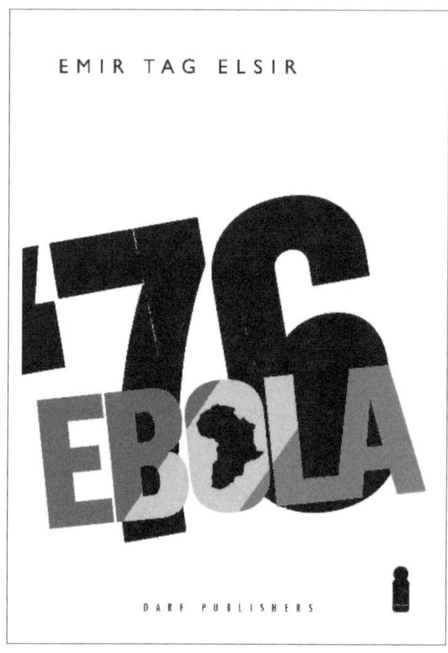

wrote *Coptic Tensions*; drawing on the events of an historical revolution, I was writing the future without realising it. The novel was published in 2009, before the time of Daesh and all the associated tragedies and atrocities – all of which is in my novel. I think the writer has a privilege no one else has, to interrogate the future, just like the past.

Similarly, I wrote *Ebola '76* in 2012, which was inspired by a sad story I had been told in 1992 by a doctor from the South when he was working for a Red Crescent clinic in Port Sudan. I was going to visit him, to look for quinine supplies that were used to treat patients who didn't respond to traditional treatments. His condition for giving up the doses I would take from him was that, in exchange, I hear his story. I learned that this doctor had been present during the first outbreak of the Ebola virus in the Congo and South Sudan in 1976. His story stayed with me until it emerged in 2012, completed and transformed by a fantasy running parallel to reality. This was also a reading of the future, since Ebola returned in 2014 with the same severity described in my novel.

Imagination is my primary guide. I try to tether it to reality, but I can't always keep hold of it. Sometimes it breaks loose and engineers varied surprises. It is with imagination that I am able to prophesy, although I don't quite know how I do it. When I go back to my novel *Ra'ashaat al-Janoub*, which was written years before the partition of Sudan, I find the history of partition there. The truth astounds me, but my astonishment soon dissipates when I remember that a novelist has a strange, and prognostic sensitivity.

A lot has been written about Port Sudan. It's always the setting that comes to mind when I start writing an urban work. I was born in North Sudan but spent most of my childhood and early teens in

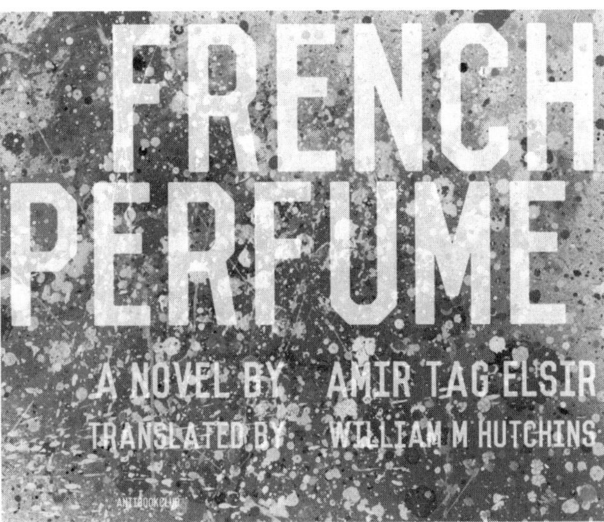

Port Sudan. I also worked as a doctor in its old hospitals and opened my clinics in its outlying districts, including al-Mirghaniyah, Slalab, and al-Nour. When I'm writing, I see the old streets, the old neighbourhoods. I see the cinema that's now closed, the clubs that have disappeared, the houses of clay, tin and wood whose appearance has evolved with the changing of the world. I even see the red light districts, which used to exist, where most of the girls were Ethiopians. All this comes to mind. It's a city that still stands and it's legitimate to write about it when I describe the seventies and eighties, the two periods of my novels *366* and *Muntaja' al-Sahiraat* (The Witches' Resort). It took a lot of courage to discuss all the recent changes – political, economic and social – in novels like *The Grub Hunter*, *French Perfume*, and *Qalam Zeinab* (Zeinab's Pen) which told the story of one of my clinics in the poor al-Nour district.

When I remember that clinic, I laugh a lot. That was how I remembered it in 2010, when I wrote *Zeinab's Pen*, the story of Idris Ali, a swindler who cast his net around me and weighed me down for a full year. I couldn't quite grasp him and when I finally got hold of him, I found he had been an inmate for years in the town of Suakin near Port Sudan. I don't know how he escaped, to torment me and then return to his prison. My experience at that clinic was highly significant; that was when I got to know characters like Ali Gargaar, whom I would use in my novel *French Perfume*, and the transgender Atif, who would come into another work, and so on.

No doubt, there now follow questions on my practices: how do you write a novel? Once questions of characters and style are settled, you've soaked up the environment and all the necessary influences, how do you bring them all together in a creative work?

The truth is that every writer is different and sometimes each book by the same author can be different. I'm the type that if I come across an idea, or a beginning I think is good, then I'll sit down and write every day until I have a completed text. I don't, and can't bear to write for years and be distracted by other things. So long as I have a piece of work in mind, I'll keep thinking about it and won't be able to think much about other normal things.

I always start with a concept that I think is special, then I search for an appropriate beginning for it until one comes to me. Then I sit and write. I don't plan and I never lay out the plot or design characters who will play a role in the work. All I do is write and write every day. Each day I read what I wrote the day before and then continue. New characters might arrive, old characters might depart. A character might die before playing a significant role, like Al-Nabawi who dies early on in *French Perfume*. A character might have all the traits of death but still live and go on, like Adam Nadhir in *The Yelling Dowry*, or Mikhael the Coptic in *Coptic Tensions*. I never think about the ending, it just comes by itself; when I reach it, I re-read my text and that's when I work consciously to arrange it if I feel it is jumbled or needs a few additions or edits.

I write in the day, from 8am until midday. I write about a thousand words a day, never more, even if it's flowing well. It gives me a strange sense of satisfaction, as well as exhaustion, probably because writing uses up so much mental energy. I usually sit in a public place in the corner of a mid-range hotel in Doha. I have written almost all of my works there. I'm consumed by my writing, despite the noise and being disturbed by the waitresses or the woman who plays the piano all day long. I might stop a little and exchange greetings if someone approaches me, but I must reach a thousands words every day until I'm content. I leave my corner at 12 noon and go to my other work as a doctor, which is always in the afternoons. The next day, I keep going until the text is finished. This could take a month or two, or longer depending on the length it reaches autonomously, without any intervention from me.

Smoking used to inspire me, or so I thought in the past. But I gave it up in recent years and nothing has changed. I have continued writing with the same perseverance and endurance, and don't think about cigarettes. It was a huge lie and I was swept up in it, until the smoking stopped but the writing didn't. Now I have tea or coffee, but nothing else.

Among the things both positive and negative that I feel at these times, is that I often suffer from depression while I'm writing. I don't know why but I get anxious and dejected, and I'm quickly irritated by the slightly provocation. The writing is intense and focused when these symptoms are at their worst. But they all go away when I finish. It's a period my family know well and they fear how agitated I can get during the periods when I'm writing. That's why I really don't like writing, but I just have to do it. As I always say, it's a kind of affliction that strikes some people, and there's no cure for it.

I'll say a little about my relationship with my readers, since they have had a big impact on me. How often have I been furious with a reader who I felt hadn't understood? And how often have I been delighted by the opinion of another whom I felt grasped what I wanted to say? The most important thing about my interaction with my readers is the letters they send me, in which they pose fascinating questions that can lead to new inspiration. This is what happened with my most recent novel, *Zuhoor Takuluha an-Nar* (Flowers eaten by Fire), which is about captives of the religious and sectarian wars in the Arab world, especially the captives of Daesh. These stories are well known but I wrote allegories for them. A female reader had come across *Coptic Tensions* and she wrote to me saying that in that book I had written about everything a man might suffer, but nothing about women. Her question stayed with me and inspired *Flowers eaten by Fire*, which is written from the perspective of Khamila the Coptic, Mikhael's fiancée and a student of aesthetics who finds herself captive, and enslaved in a house with other women.

I've given here a brief summary of my experience, both good and bad, and the impact it has had in developing and determining things for me. I'm happy to say that many of the works that have been translated into other languages (like *Ebola '76*, *The Grub Hunter* and *French Perfume*) have done well overseas. This inspires me enormously to continue.

TRANSLATED BY JULIA IHNATOWICZ

GUEST POET
ANGEL GUINDA

Banipal 59's guest author is the great Spanish poet Àngel Guinda. The feature opens with an introduction by Trinidad Ruiz Marcellàn, the founder and director of Olifante Ediciones de Poesía, the publisher of Guinda's collections, followed by poems, translated by the award-winning translator Peter Bush.

Àngel Guinda was born in Zaragoza, Spain, in 1948. Since the late 1960s he has been writing poetry, essays and articles on literature and other subjects, editing major anthologies of Spanish poetry, teaching, and translating Italian and Portuguese-language poets into Spanish. He lives in Madrid.

His poetry includes the important collections *Vida ávida*, *Claro interior* and *Materia del amor*, amongst many others, in addition to his essays *El mundo del poeta, el poeta en el mundo* (The world of the poet, the poet in the world) and *La experiencia de la poesía* (The experience of poetry).

He won the Aragonese Literature Prize in 2010, and was short-listed for the Critics' Prize in 2012 and the National Poetry Prize in 2013 with his books *Espectral* and *Caja de larva*, respectively.

Milan 2017. Photo by Samuel Shimon

TRINIDAD RUIZ MARCELLÁN

The poetry of Angel Guinda

Angel Guinda is recognised as "one of the most necessary and original poets in Spanish literature in recent decades"[i] and "one of the most important living poets on active service"[ii].

I have known and worked with him for fifty years and have been publishing his poetry for forty. I collect the articles and studies critics publish about him. His personality is forged from a series of contrasts. In respect of others and his temperament, Ángel is straightforward, friendly, direct, transparent, enthusiastic, talkative, compassionate, generous, tolerant, hedonist, supportive and amusing. As regards himself he seems complex, solitary, resigned, melancholy, introverted, austere, hardworking, demanding, perfectionist and tragic. His life and work have been marked by the death of his mother when she was giving birth to him.

His poetry is harsh and profound in content, clear and aphoristic in form. It is born from visceral feelings, a sense of responsibility, brutal experiences, a calming imagination and memories that can never be erased. It displays authenticity, knowledge, didacticism, tension and intensity. The main phases in its development have been bitter realism, critical consciousness, constant reflection, and the illumination almost of a seer.

With "an incorruptible voice"[iii], "with a trajectory that should be arrayed alongside our most significant poets outside the mainstream"[iv], Guinda's poetry has sustained "a radical coherence in its evolution"[v], beyond the dominant aesthetic tendencies within Spain. A coherence that derives from that constructive destruction, a characteristic of *poètes maudits* (a feature noted by Ángel Crespo, Leopoldo de Luis, Germán Labrador Méndez or Marta Sanz Pastor, and others), that is a feature of Romanticism (according to Manuel Martínez Forega and Labrador Méndez), "with a belligerent attitude towards the financial and political powers-that-be"[vi], opposed to reality, rebellious before the world, from which he feels exiled: "I don't want to live in this world", he confesses.

As regards the poet's first creative phase, Crespo was of the opinion that "Ángel Guinda has erupted in the concert – disconcertingly for some – of Spanish poetry with a voice that is as personal as it is unnerving, and which has surprised critics astonished by his re-writing of post-war poetic values [...] Guinda's poetry is shocking, and its author a *maudit*. He himself states that the poet is 'a man condemned to clarity and song', and preaches the destruction that must necessarily precede the new order he dreams of, conscious of the mission he feels driven to carry out – from the shadows and the margins, like all great rebels – he exclaims: 'I will leave all I have lived/ and I will live for me, for you, with everyone /.../ As you must die, live your life!' This poet, who states he has been incinerated, 'because he was fuel and fire' is one of those who rebelled in the Seventies, as the surrealists and *postistas* of the Forties and Fifties rebelled against the subsidiary species of realism that comprises the most conservative wing of post-war Spanish poetry. He says that explicitly when he states 'I write against reality, not about it', and when he warns 'Don't look at what you see but at what blinds you'.

"But I don't think any of this really upsets conventional critics, rather it is Ángel Guinda's use of direct, sometimes colloquial, language. He has managed to be intoxicated by alcohol, drugs, sex and poetry, but has never consequently renounced his prophetic tone that heralds a salutary longing for life. *Maudit* as poet and prophet."[vii]

Manuel Martínez Forega suggests that "Romanticism never fails to refer to fantasy, dreams, imagination, originality as transcendental elements inspiring creation. It reiterates the value of feelings, of emotion, of the values that live in the heart next to all that life pours into the poem.

When the poet evokes these principles, he associates them with a state of exultation and euphoria: a kind of inebriation. And, indeed, as the author of *Inner Light* demands: 'Make your heart a tavern open…'."[viii]

Germán Labrador Méndez also underlines the romantic aspect: "openly romantic, he accentuates his darts as a *maudit* . . . In *Avid Life* satanism, licentiousness, and drug addiction are just a few of the zones where the call of evil acts as ascesis, a counterpoint to the hagiographical horizon of Francoist morality".[ix]

Marta Sanz Pastor notes: "'The best of life' is a poem from *Knowledge of the Medium*. One of the blurbs points out: 'it is an act of reflection applied to temporal and biographical space that is shown as the only space there is, as all the beautiful tempests of youth are already decanted in memory, the expression of a reality that recapitulates everything else: 'All lives work towards death'. Gamoneda emphasises Guinda's expressive straightforwardness and above all his features that 'are radically, overwhelmingly lived'".[x]

Pablo Luque Pinilla reminds us that this poetry "tackles life, time and death […] from a concern for the human that it exacerbates to the point of lesion, to the implosion of the poetic subject […] and is sustained by three fundamental ideas: poetry as an act of destruction, the conviction that 'you write as you live' and the awareness of the marginal nature of anyone who exalts the quest for profound lyricism, thus condemning himself to enlighten the world […] We believe it is right to see that *mauditisme* as the shadow the temptation of self-absorption casts over his work […] towards a poetry on the path to mystery."[xi]

I would like finally to stress the way that Guinda connects poetically to the multiverse or plurality of universes, from the vibration, intuition and discovery of the quantic world to uncertainty and happenstance.

TRANSLATED FROM
THE SPANISH BY PETER BUSH

ANGEL GUINDA

Selected poems

TRANSLATED FROM THE SPANISH BY PETER BUSH

DESERT

I walk
on torches
of silence.
I hear shadows:
they are the footsteps of the sun.

WHAT A YOUNGSTER HEARD

You, who interpret suicidal eyes
in their beauty full of renunciation,
make your heart a tavern open
from dusk to dawn to all who suffer,
seeking stars in a pit of slime.
And attack life the aggressor.

L.S.D.

Labyrinth of Diabolical Solitude.
Escape will not be possible.
Your mother's murderer, trafficker in death,
condemned eternally not to give life
not to avoid fresh crimes,
you need to live, to live more,
for yourself and all the unborn.

Tortured,
you will never be free of this anguish.
When you love, you will hate.
Only the day when you destroy all laws
will you enjoy the magic of your rebellion,
and attain peace, pissing
on your father's grave
to fertilise his death.
My caricature curses your character.
Against walls and horizons.
Die!

CLOSING IN ON LUCIFER

An inner magnet cries out,
between columns of red-hot crystal,
that there are chance crypts
where enigmatic petals of blue wax
enjoy war on Cain,
glorious Lucifer and Prometheus
equally intoxicated on solar chalices.
Clinging to red tunics of rebellion
I will not ignore
the demon's voice.
I will be reconciled with the light.
Gods, show me the faces of hell!

TREASURE

In this life, you always search for what
you think was lost in other lives.
Nobody knows what it might be,
and everybody would give almost anything
to find it within themselves.
But the light is too bright,
the deadline too short.

I HAVE SMOKED MY LIFE AWAY

I have smoked my life away
as time has smoked me.
Look at this larynx, this trachea,
these bronchiole and lungs
machine-gunned by nicotine.
I have smoked subterranean gases
on Metro platforms;
the air of Madrid, filthy
betrayal of the loveliest light;
the plaster blizzards on slate,
the black bonfire of exhaust pipes,
the dry leaves of marijuana,
the asphalt, the fog, the damp,
the soft almonds of clitoris,
the sinister trail of atoms
when I fled my shadow,
and my life turned to dust,
and the dust I will become
beneath the secret tree of death.

THE GOLDEN AGE

Don't regret
losing the splendours of youth,
the explosions of life,
in exchange
for a horizon of ashes.
Nobody can advance through
a wood in flames,
a desert, for sure.

IN RESPONSE TO A YOUNG GIRL

With age Goya's palette darkens.

With age one starts to shed
ballast; one loses height, hearing, hair, memory,
drive and even the desire to travel.

With age you become less
suspicious of everyone and almost everything, nothing
shocks you, you expect no miracles and
suspect you too will die.

With age you sleep less and less,
suffer more paranoias, disappointments and fears.

With age everything degenerates: the
world collapses.

But don't you worry, this only happens with
age.

SMOKE RINGS

I tried to pin the world down with words:
I was trapped by them.
I sought out words like worlds:
I went silent.
Without world or words,
in the smoke, I pursue light.

DYING

Dying is not being
at the same time
in the same places

with the same people.
Not appearing, every morning,
like that bright new light
scattered over things;
leaving tasks unfinished,
journeys at a dead end.
Alien to the seas and the stars.
Dying is being still, deaf,
blind, mute, disappeared,
disconnected from everyone and everything,
from ourselves even;
never ever returning home.
No longer giving out signals,
or receiving any.
Dying is not going back.

ANOTHER LIGHT

Lit in the light is another light.
The obscure within the visible.

THE SEA

My head is a sea surrounded by mountains
where the silence roars
and clouds rest like dead gulls.
My head is a sea among scaffolds of fog
or the great dust cloud from demolition jobs.
My head is a sea.
A sea whose windows tremble like lightning strikes,
and over its waves resound echoes of the sun.
My head is a sea of silt and labyrinths
where horses of the air shake their manes.
My head is a sea. And volcanoes in flames
harbour in its ports, memories anguished.

My head is the sea of detonations,
of smoking goodbye drums and their ruins.
My head is a sea
or the book that lists the collapses,
heaven's rubbish, the lost treasure.
My head is a sea.
My head is a sea of ambushes and tunnels,
avalanches of light and fissures of drought.
Turmoil without motion, my head is a sea.
My head is a sea at the bottom of which scream
watery suicides, boats and planes
shot down by the horizon.
My head is a sea and, on its beaches, children
play at spotting sweets of fire drop
from wars in a world which is not mine.
My head is the sea where I have been shipwrecked.

NO

I am a bright interior, the future
of a door that is always barred,
trapped in life and in sight of death.

Against the destruction of consciousness
I scream, I erupt, I sink my elbows into God.
I lash out, my patience gone.

A light that, scraping the debris,
erases the fog and goes forward.
A soul with shadows up to its shoulders.

I eat hunger and drink thirst with all
those condemned to scour the void.
This is no poem, it's an insult.

Loudly I proclaim a deafening no.
I do not want to live in this world.

BOXES

A native would say this and she'd be right.
"You organise your lives in boxes.
You are born, and are put in a little box,
your house is a box, and the rooms
are smaller boxes.
You go up in a box,
you go down in a box.
You travel in a box.
You sleep and make love on a box.
You move house: you put everything in boxes.
Banks have strong-boxes and tick boxes.
And when you die
they put you in another box."
Everything is made to box us.
They box in our lives.
Some of us won't be boxed and we de-box.

WRITING

If they rob me of words, I will write in silence.
If they rob me of light, I will write in shadows.
If I lose my memory, I will invent another oblivion.
If they halt the sun, clouds, and planets,
I will start to gyrate.
If they silence music, I will sing without a voice.
If they burn paper, if inks go dry,
if computer screens shatter,
if they demolish words, I will write with my breath.
If they extinguish the fire that ignites me,
I will write in smoke.
And when smoke doesn't exist,
I will write in the gazes born without my eyes.
If they rob me of life, I will write in death.

[AS A BOY IN ZARAGOZA I SAW . . .]

As a boy in Zaragoza I saw rhinoceroses with
men's heads, men with pistol
heads, men with phallus heads, men
with ciborium heads, men with
rams' heads, oxen's heads, shrunken
heads; big-headed, heady men, men
with heads for feet. Sheep with women's
heads, women with cot heads, women
with doe heads, women with stove
heads, women with dragon
heads, with virgin, with
holocaust heads; women
with heads of mercy, women with
their heads in their hands. Herds of woman
and men with heads without eyes, mouths, ears
and noses. Headless men and women.
And heads rolling down
the street.

[I WANT TO DIE STANDING . . . !

I want to die standing, as trees die!

THE BOTTLE

The sea fits in this bottle.
The sky totters,
the suns of drunkards totter
truth on their shoulders,
in this bottle,
sickened by bitterness.
Flies dance in this bottle
like helicopters under fire,

cockroaches stroll under umbrellas.
Absence rains in this bottle.
its rotating wall disfigures my faces,
sags my temples, opens my pupils:
storms of axes clash in its magma.
In this bottle is the void
I fill up on when I drink and drink.
Relegated for recycling,
I am this bottle.

THE EMIGRANTS

Immigrants walk along the streets with shrouds on their shoulders,
gravestones on their shoulders, crosses on their shoulders, tears on
their shoulders, hearts in their hand, the sky over a
desert in their gaze. A family and a country
inside their head.
Immigrants have many shoulders, many
hearts, many hands, many legs.
They go into shops, into banks, into telephone booths,
into bars: with framed photos under one
arm, coffins under the other.
Nobody sees those shrouds, those gravestones, those crosses,
those tears, those hearts, those families, those countries,
those photographs, those coffins, skies or deserts.
They don't look into our eyes: they have seen our blindness!

CRUCIFIXION

I speak in the name of those whose life is a
crossroads!

In the name of those who only find crosses at each

step, scarecrows on crosses, crucifixes on their
pilgrimages.

I speak in the name of those who hardly make any headway
rebounding off crosses, moving crosses aside, dodging
tombs, knocked down by crosses.

Women and men without a voice, their hands crossed!

Crosses errant across stony fields.

I speak for the crucified!

Am I a †?

I am the crucifixion!

How can I cross my arms
and watch the world turn carrying so many crosses?

WHAT'S LEFT OF ALL THAT

You are impossibly possible.
You are the air around me.
You are the orbit I circle.
You are what initiates mystery.
You are the absence that accompanies.
You are sun that freezes me.
You are the earthquake's prayer.
You are the root raising me.
You are the light of each night.
You are the magnet trapping me.
You are the glacier burning me.
You are what fills the void.
You are the silence speaking to me.
You are the invisibly visible.
You are the echo from the abyss.
You are what's left of all that!

AND

I'm no longer breathless.

(Now I breathe your breath.)

By your side

I thirst for fire, not water.

By your side

everything disappears except you.

(I leave the world when I enter you.)

DIFFERENCE

Everything harmonises through difference:
the desert on ice, the tree on the rock,
the gently raging sea and stars.
We are born transparent like the air,
we become opaque like marble.
One tolerates as much pain
as pleasure one receives.
Stone, grass, fire, water,
light, shadows, sandstorm:
everything harmonises through difference.
The city, while you sleep,
dredges the silence, makes everything anew.
Cloud, root, bird song:
everything harmonises through difference.

THE DEAD

The hands of absence reach out far
till they clasp the world of the dead:
the dead living us,
the dead killing us,
the dead paying us a visit,
the living dead,
the dead calling to us,
the dead dying again,
the dead awaiting us in death.

GOLDSMITHS

I cannot cut the air.
I cannot cut the water.
I cannot cut the light.
I will make pearls from silence.

Notes:

i Saldaña, Alfredo, "Las huellas de Ángel Guinda", *Clarín: revista de nueva literatura*, Year IV, nº 20, March-April 1999, pp. 84-85.

ii Escarpa, Gonzalo. *Literalia Tv*. "Todo es poesía menos la poesía", chapter 10.

iii García Jambrina, Luis, "Una voz insobornable", *ABC* "Cultural", Madrid, 29 December 20007, p. 17.

iv Rico, Manuel, "Espectral / Caja de lava" *El País*, "Babelia", Madrid, 14 April 2002, p. 10.

v Valcárcel, Xulio, "La llegada del mal tiempo, de A. Guinda", *El Ideal Gallego*, 22 August 1999.

vi Jiménez Domínguez, Jesús, *Revista Turia*.

vii Crespo, Ángel. "Ángel Guinda, poeta maldito", *Revista Brasilia*, included in *Las cenizas de la flor* (pp.233-240)).

viii Martínez Forega, Manuel. "Un Claustro romántico. (Aproximación al Romanticismo en la poesía de Ángel Guinda)", in *El desierto sacudido (Actas del Curso Poesía aragonesa contemporánea)*, Zaragoza, Government of Aragón, Collection Actas, Zaragoza, 1998, pp.289-324.

Ix Sanz Pastor, Marta. "Ángel Guinda", en *Antología de la poesía española (1966-2000): Metalingüísticos y sentimentales*, Madrid, Biblioteca Nueva, 2007, pp. 328-336.

x Luque Pinilla, Pablo. "Ángel Guinda", in *Avanti: Poetas españoles de entresiglos XX-XXI*, Zaragoza,Olifante Ediciones de Poesía, 2009, pp. 77-9

The Longlist

The eight novels in the following feature were longlisted for the International Prize for Arabic Fiction (IPAF) in 2016 and 2017. Over a number of years Banipal has introduced, in collaboration with IPAF, many of the shortlisted authors. We decided that in this issue we would introduce longlisted authors as our focus theme

Photo: Ahmed Ben Ismail

YASSIN ADNAN

Hot Maroc

EXCERPTS FROM THE NOVEL
TRANSLATED BY
RAPHAEL COHEN

Hot Maroc is a novel about the changing face of Morocco: about Marrakech and the effects of ruralisation, the university and its student movement, internet cafés and hackers, daily life and human nature, politics and journalism, and bizarre election campaigns in a country where people do not vote. It is about Rahal Laaouina, the slow-witted coward who becomes a hero in his dreams and online, whether on facebook or the news site called *Hot Maroc*.

The Squirrel Enters the Blue Box

6

The King is Dead! Long Live the King! Long live the multi-ringtone mobile. Long live modern technology! Long live the blue screen!

When the people in sore need of God devote themselves to the mobile and set off into the kingdom of the electron, their need is forgotten. The world becomes a small village, at the fingertips of the population in the internet cafés that have spread like a rash at democratic prices. No price rises for the poor! Two dirhams for a quick visit. Three dirhams for half an hour; five for a full hour. For loyal customers the second hour is four dirhams, and so on. A few dirhams and a few words of a foreign language and God's online people can roam the polyglot pavilions of the blonde. That's for males. For females, clunky Arabic suffices to make red-blooded connected hearts leap from the Atlantic to the Gulf.

Long live technology!

As for Rahal, aka Nomad, aka Squirrel, he was at the heart of it . . . the right place at the right time.

He opened a Hotmail account, not to mail anyone but just to have a Hotmail account. He set up another on Maktoob, not to chat with Arabs online, but because naturally he had to have a Maktoob account. The third was Yahoo, just because it was Yahoo. The fourth he still had to decide.

All the cybercafé's customers were new to the field. Most were at the stage of discovery. So whenever a newbie turned up, he asked Rahal for a computer and a helping hand. This one wanted to open a Hotmail account, another a Yahoo account. Rahal stayed up late opening online accounts for them. A new service that seemed magical to first-time visitors to the cybercafé. So he set a price of 30 dirhams. The account was free, but Rahal made 30 dirhams from every one he opened. The customers found it normal. How could it be possible to get an email account that did the same things as a PO box in Massira post office for nothing? And Rahal's mailboxes were better, since you only had to pay the sign-up fee on day one and it was open for good.

Customers came and went, taking it in turns at the computers and guiding the optical mouses over the desktops. All the same, a little family gradually coalesced around Rahal. Salim, the high-school student, dazzled by the new online world. He had two emails so far, Hotmail and Yahoo. Sometimes he came with his father, at times with his younger sister Lamia. He was always looking for sources of information online, and every day he printed out the results of his research, which he knew how to flaunt to his classmates.

Samira and Fadoua came in together, sat together, and left together. Specialists in chat rooms, they merged into a single avatar. They loved chatting to boys in Arabic, French, and English. Username: Marrakech Star.

"Two in one: shampoo and conditioner together," Qamar Eddine al-Suyuti would tease them whenever he spotted them coming into the cybercafé.

Qamar Eddine, the son of Shihab Eddine al-Suyuti, the best-known teacher of Islamic studies at Massira High School and the one most joked about by the pupils.

"Which one of us is the shampoo, and which one the conditioner?" Fadoua asked him conspiratorially.

"To be honest, I'm still not sure. When I decide you're the shampoo, I'll let you know."

Qamar Eddine knew all the tales of Marrakech Star, especially as Fadoua and Samira turned to him for all their messages in English. He explained anything unclear in people's emails and corrected their replies so they crossed the Net with fewer mistakes.

Qamar Eddine's English was good, and his French, but he always muttered, with or without cause, that unfortunately his Arabic was poor. His features displayed no sorrow when he repeated his confession. On the contrary his face almost glowed with hidden pride. Did he say it to spite Mr Shihab Eddine? The Arabic teacher who shifted to Islamic studies, not because of an upwelling of religiosity, but out of laziness and a desire to escape classes in grammar and parsing. Islamic Knowledge was not a core subject for either science or arts students. Two hours a week for everyone. Many pupils thought the class was a break and they spent it on the sportsground or in front of school or, for those who had the money, skating the glacial screen and surfing the waves of light with Rahal, particularly as Mr al-Suyuti did not take the register.

Qamar Eddine did not actually hate his father, but he hated the talking about him. He always preferred the company of friends who did not go to Massira High School and so knew nothing about the character of Mr Shihab Eddine and had not heard the jokes or funny stories about him. Fadoua and Samira were an exception. Although they had both studied with Mr al-Suyuti, their relationship with Qamar Eddine was the product of the cybercafé and had nothing to do with school. Besides, he was a handsome guy, brilliant at languages, so his friendship was win-win for the binary Marrakech Star.

Qamar Eddine was in the cybercafé constantly, so much so that Rahal left him to look after the place whenever some emergency forced him to leave or go to school to fulfil one of Hiyam's ever-urgent requests. Qamar Eddine began to take vicarious pleasure in the online adventures and conquests of the Marrakech Star in east and west. This one was serious, this one coy, and that one had honourable intentions. This one wanted to visit Marrakech because of her eyes and asked about the best hotels and suitable flights. Another proposed she come to London. He would pay the plane ticket and welcome her into his flat to spend a week with him as an esteemed and venerated guest, or for a whole month, if her precious time permitted. Another, with awesome humility, suggested they went on the lesser pilgrimage to Esteemed Mecca.

But as soon as Amelia the Nigerian's sun rose in the cybercafé, the Marrakech Star was eclipsed. Fadoua noticed that Qamar Eddine lost his concentration whenever the black Nigerian sun peeked out. Amelia sometimes came on her own, sometimes her friend Flora came too. Jackaboo always joined them afterwards. That might have been a ploy so that Rahal did not stop the three of them sitting at one screen. The rules of the place were well known: maximum two per computer.

What kind of relationship existed between Jackaboo and Amelia and Flora no one knew. Was he their brother? A relative? Or the boyfriend of one of them? It was always hard to guess with Africans. Whatever the case, they were lucky: landlords didn't ask for their papers, even if they were Muslims from Mali or Senegal. They didn't get checked out like Moroccans. Local guys had a hard time living with their girlfriends without a marriage certificate. But no one questioned Africans, so they lived together, five to ten on top of each other in a small apartment of two rooms, kitchen, and bathroom. Qamar Eddine didn't generally bother about these details. He wasn't in love with Amelia; she just made him happy. Her long neck delighted him and her smile gave him a thrill. That was enough for him. Sitting with her also gave him a good opportunity to chat in English, which she knew very well. But there was a more important reason . . . somewhat sensitive. One better not to broach near other people, especially not Fadoua and Samira.

Qamar Eddine wanted to flee the country by any means necessary. Shihab Eddine exhausted him; his boring life at home exhausted him, as did the college, which he infrequently attended, and even the bloody cybercafé, to which he seemed addicted. Rahal's snooping exhausted him. Whenever he turned round he saw the rat monitoring his screen. The discussions of his history teachers at high school exhausted him – they came en masse to the cybercafé. They did not have set times, but when they did honour the place, they did so as a group, as if they were going to mosque. They took a computer each, and rather than surfing, they started chatting as though they were in the staff room. They said life in the days of Hassan II had been worse, and the situation in the country had improved a lot with the advent of the young king, that there were margins for freedom, a new vitality, and signs of change. Qamar Eddine wasn't interested in the stories of his father's colleagues. He could see no change at all. Besides, who said he wanted to know what life had been like under Hassan II? He had been small then. Now he felt grown up and did not want to go backwards. He didn't have time to waste on such talk. He wanted another kind of life. The life he saw in films and on television. Life as lived by God's chosen people in the North. Qamar Eddine wanted to run away from here. Migration was a sacred right. He did not understand why he had to stay in a place where non-entities he did not like suffocated him. He did not understand why he did not have the right to force this whole tedious world out of his days and nights, out of his life and future, and set off.

7

"Christian of course. Why do you ask?" replied Amelia.

"Just asking. But can we talk outside?"

She left Flora on her own glued to the screen, excusing herself in a local Nigerian dialect that meant Qamar Eddine only gathered Jackaboo's name, which she repeated three times. Outside, he invited her to the Milano café opposite the cyber. He discovered that Amelia smoked. As soon as the waitress Asmaa place a cup of coffee in front of her, Amelia took a pack of Marquise out of her pocket, lit a cigarette, and offered the pack to Qamar Eddine.

"Thanks. I don't smoke . . . I won't keep you long, but I'd like to learn about Christianity from you. I mean I'd like to know more. I read online about the Trinity and the oneness of God, about the divine nature of Lord Jesus, and his humanity, about the difference between Orthodox Christianity and Catholicism, and then about Protestants and Anglicans. I've also read the Sermon on the Mount dozens of times and learnt bits of it in Arabic, French, and English by heart. Want to be sure? Try this: 'You have heard that it was said, "An eye for an eye and a tooth for a tooth." But I say to you, 'Do not resist one who is evil. But if any one strikes you on the right cheek, turn to him the other. And if anyone wants . . . anyone wants . . .' See I've forgotten. There's another passage after it that goes: 'You have heard that it was said, "You shall love your neighbour and hate your enemy." But I say to you, "Love your enemies and pray for those who persecute you, so that you may be sons of your Father who is in heaven; for he makes his sun rise on the evil and on the good, and sends rain on the just and on the unjust."' There's also, "Seek and you shall find" that I've learnt by heart. Listen . . .'

"No, you listen, Qamar . . . "

"Abdel Massih. My new name is Abdel Massih (Servant of the Messiah). You're the first person I've told. It's our secret."

"Listen, Abdel Massih, it seems there's been some confusion. When I told you I was Christian, I was talking in general about the family faith. But trust me, I'm not a Christian in the sense you mean. I don't go to church, and don't read the Bible, and haven't memorized the Sermon on the Mount. A Christian, that's all. Take it from me like that. And let's go back to the cyber, please. Flora's waiting for me."

Qamar Eddine was disappointed. In fact, he had discovered Christianity by chance. It started with surfing porn sites. Because the rat staying up at the place was lashing his back with curious hungry looks, he started browsing sites about migration. He left that to parkour through cyberspace. One more big leap and without premeditation he found himself on the opposite shore as a follower of Jesus Christ: "'Teacher, I will follow you wherever you go.' And Jesus said to him, 'Foxes have holes, and birds of the air have nests; but the Son of man has nowhere to lay his head.'"

I have believed, my Teacher. The Son of man has nowhere to lay his head.

Qamar Eddine was stunned by Amelia's cold response. He was in dire need for someone to support him at that critical time in his online search for the truth. Amelia was his black angel, his father who art in cyberspace. His mother. His sister. It made no difference. Her smile revealed the patience of the saints to him. But she had disappointed him in a way that really hurt. Imagine, she did not read the Bible and had not memorized the Sermon on the Mount!

Amelia, however, was shocked. Since they started visiting the cybercafé Flora and Jackaboo had pointed out to her that Qamar Eddine had fallen for her, or was at least clearly interested. She had been watching him since then. She liked the way he looked and loved his wisecracks, his sense of humour and charm, his excellent English, and his polite way of talking to everyone. Why not? A nice guy who deserved her attention. Amelia was ready for anything with Qamar Eddine, from burning love to passing fling. When he invited her to the café that afternoon, she went out with him happy and eager. Then the idiot dragged her into a heavy conversation about the Trinity and the Sermon on the Mount. Amelia knew about Qamar Eddine's obsession with emigrating, but had never imagined that his craziness would end up with him thinking about Christianity as an excuse to leave the country. Besides, she was a Christian from generations of Christians. Surely, when it came to going to Europe, if precedence were given to followers of Lord Jesus, she would have headed straight there from Lagos, esteemed and venerated, and not have endured the long trek across the Sahara before finding herself and her companions trapped in Morocco. They had not been lucky enough to slip into Spain, and they weren't able to go back to their country and face their family and friends with their failure, after squandering the family's money on the long and arduous journey.

8

Qamar Eddine seemed to enjoy the role of everybody's friend at the cybercafé. He fluttered from one computer to another like an e-butterfly. One moment helping Salim to do his homework, one moment helping Fadoua and Samira to interpret an email that had just arrived in Marrakech Star's Hotmail inbox. Sometimes he took Rahal's place when he was out, and sometimes he would exchange whispers with Jackaboo once he discovered that the Nigerian guy was more religious than his two female companions.

Abdel Massih's polar opposite was Abu Qatada.

He talked to no one. He stepped into the cybercafé with his right leg first, reciting the Verses of Refuge. Bidding "peace upon you" to all Muslims was indeed a duty, but Abu Qatada found it hard to raise his voice and bid peace whenever he went into the cybercafé and he found the two half-naked Jezebels with that pandering pimp, called erroneously and falsely the shining "Moon of Faith" – Qamar Eddine.

"Who's that Qamar Eddine? That Qamar of shit. Moon of Misfortune, not Moon of Faith. God curse the day he was born."

Abu Qatada was careful to keep his distance from the Africans. While it might be true that "there is no distinction between Arab and foreigner, or white and black, except in piety," yet the Africans' dark faces did not intimate modesty or radiate piety. Not because they were black, God forbid. Our lord Bilal, the muezzin of the Prophet – upon him the most fragrant praise and peace – was an Ethiopian slave. Islam honoured him to the extent that the beloved Prophet described him as one of the men of Paradise and said of him, "Blessed be the man Bilal. He is lord of the muezzins. And the necks of the muezzins will be held high on the Day of Judgment." Abu Qatada noticed that Jackaboo's neck was long and slender like a giraffe's. "But his dusky face could not be further from radiating the light of Islam. He and his two hideous slave girls, who never seem to leave him. They look like two goats. Damn him and them," thought Abu Qatada, then asked God to forgive him.

Abu Qatada's real name was Mahjoub Didi, a civil servant at RADEEMA, the local water and electricity utility. He was married with two children. What most wound him up was a boorish colleague at work teasing him with the song "Didi, Didi, Didi, Wah." His unpleasantness made his colleagues afraid to sing Cheb Khaled's famous song in front of him, but they joked about it in his absence. The nickname Abu Qatada had been chosen by one of the brethren – God reward him – at a perfumed Dhikr. From that day, his name in divine assemblies and on effulgent websites was Abu Qatada, after the glorious companion of the Prophet, Abu Qatada al-Ansari al-Khazraji, may God be pleased with him and grant him satisfaction.

9

Big Brother is watching you!

Qamar Eddine repeated this phrase from time to time in mocking reference to Rahal.

"Sorry, sorry, I meant to say: Little brother is watching you!" and the cyber burst into laughter.

It must be admitted that Rahal's English was almost non-existent, while his knowledge of English literature was not much greater than Amelia's knowledge of the doctrine of Imam Malik. Anyhow, Rahal was in the department of Arabic literature, specialising in classical poetry, the Hanging Odes, Umayyad and Abbasid poetry, Andalusian and Moroccan. But novels he did not read, even in Arabic in which he was fluent, to spell them out in other languages. Because no one had explained to him the connection with George Orwell's *1984*, where Big Brother watches everyone, Rahal always wondered, "Why does Qamar Eddine always crow about his brothers, the big one and the little one, in the cybercafé, though he's only got one sister, who's at college in Rabat?"

Little brother is watching you!

Qamar Eddine's hinting at what Rahal was doing did not make the Squirrel budge an inch. Qamar Eddine objected to the way Rahal thought the monitors of customers in the place were his and had not the slightest shame about fixing his rodent eyes on them. That pissed Qamar Eddine off a lot during the early stages of his virtual life when he was still addicted to porn sites. Till now, he hated anyone spying on his blessed websites. So he took to avoiding pages with images of churches, icons, and religious paintings. Mostly, he copied and pasted the text onto a neutral blank document and read at his leisure in Word. Once he was done, he would delete the file and leave.

However, in the kingdom of the little bastard Rahal, the Recycle Bin had no use. After the last customer had left at midnight, Rahal spent a few minutes, which might stretch to an hour, checking the computers. He went through them one by one, delving deep into their inner workings to wrench out the secrets of those who had gone into the digital dark. Many left their email or chat accounts open. Brother Abu Qatada, for example, after hearing the call to evening prayer would call it quits and go, leaving the forum open and the discussion with the brethren ongoing. Sometimes about the duty to kill and sacrifice oneself if Muslim lands should fall under occupation; another time about the corruption of elections as a way to reach power and obtain office. Discussion was heated that time, as always when it came to elections. God's Brotherhood were vigorously opposed to the heresy of candidates putting themselves forward and the idea that all members of society had equal voting rights, whatever their level of knowledge or piety. When it came to Abdel Massih's learning and his chapters of the Gospel, Rahal restored them from the trash, and copied the Arabic material to his own computer to look over at leisure the following day.

These extra efforts of Rahal came before he locked up. It had been him who had first opened email accounts for the members of the club. His squirrel's memory retained all the user names, real and assumed, and passwords. The barriers were lifted, the secrets unveiled. That little bastard Rahal knew everything about the subjects of his happy cyber kingdom. Even the secrets of the Nigerian community at the Atlas Lion Cubs cybercafé were uncovered once their activities moved online. Amelia and Flora were two lesbians from the tribe of Lot, but worked as prostitutes with men for the moment, as they waited to penetrate the emerging and promising women's market in Marrakech. Jackaboo worked as their companion, bodyguard, and intermediary. His relationship with Flora was camouflage, Qamar Eddine, just camouflage.

Yes, Rahal, mate, you can see them moving before you like marionettes, unaware that all of them are in your pocket. Their real names and their assumed ones. Their surface appearance and their hidden depths. Their dreams and their fantasies. Their nonsense and their games. Their innocent cyber friendships and their sluttish online adventures. Everything in your pocket, Rahal. Now you have to step up your behaviour. Be extra vigilant that these secrets remain under wraps. Keep them to yourself, you weak little Squirrel. Otherwise, if Abu Qatada for example knew that Qamar Eddine had deviated from his guided path and left the community and religion to change his name to Abdel Massih, and that the two Nigerians were girls of the night, he would declare Jihad on the spot and a vicious war would break out in the cybercafé. For this reason, Rahal enjoyed spying on the members of his new family, while being careful to give every one of them a complete sense of security. Besides, they were really at home in the bosom of their happy family here in this virtual jungle of the Atlas Lion Cubs cybercafé.

10

There's the rest, then there's *Hot Maroc*.

Hot Maroc.

That was the name of the website.

An online newspaper covering events hour by hour. All the country's news fresh and tasty: politics, business and finance, sport, arts, travel and tourism, religion and fatwas, international stories, the regions, protests and sit-ins, public freedoms, crime, behind the scenes of politics and society, opinion pieces, heated debates, exclusive scoops, and also, culture has news.

Rahal started the day with Hot Maroc reports. The first thing he did after unlocking the place and switching on the computers was open the fab online newspaper that had restored his interest in public affairs. Rahal, someone who had never once bought a printed newspaper. Since quitting the Moroccan National Union of Students meetings at college he was completely cut off. All he knew was the hedgehog (his wife) and her prick, the pelican (his Mum) and the mantis (his Dad) and the monotony of their lethargic life at his Uncle Ayyad's house, where the Abadi tribal trio ate and awaited death. Hiyam and her laughable ever-urgent errands (she even sent him winging it to the women's bathhouse once because she'd forgotten her phone there). That surrogate family that had him surrounded and which he himself surrounded, that kept a close eye on him, and on which he kept a close eye here at the cyber.

Hot Maroc was Rahal's free ticket back to his country. Just like an emigrant gone for years overseas who had lost all touch with news of home. Now he was finally back, without having to buy a ticket, fascinated with the affairs and despairs of the country.

Breaking.

Scoop.

Exclusive.

There was always some breaking news story at the top of the home page. And breaking news kept coming. Hot like bread straight out of the oven. Fresh like a fish hooked from the depths. Rahal was addicted to the newspaper's fresh loaves and fishes. He took another hit at the top of the hour when he checked for more breaking news.

Hot Maroc was not just an online newspaper for Rahal. It was a space for free expression and mudslinging. His new toilet. When he noticed the comments section, initially he couldn't believe it. Below every article or story was a space for comments. Amazing. Rahal, you can write whatever you want without the stink reaching your nostrils. Comment at leisure from the comfort of your desk, not with your knees clenched to your stomach while you squeeze out your guts in the toilet. You can interact with what you read from right here in the Atlas Lion Cubs cybercafé in Massira. You can say your piece freely and anonymously with nobody asking for your name or title. Look at the list of comments: full real names, others just a first name like Karim, Khaled, Mona, Saeed. Signatures referring to cities or regions: Samira the Marrakechi, Farid from Meknes, Casablancan, Sefrou_Kid, The Sahraoui, Free Amazigh, Daughter of the North. Just write your name and email, and comment as you please.

Rahal was ecstatic when he read his first comment that appeared a few minutes after posting. It was on an opinion piece about elections and democracy in Morocco and the Arab world by the Moroccan intellectual Essam Louzi. The article tried to explain how "in the Arab world we equate elections and democracy, although as a matter of logic the part does not equal the whole nor does the means equal the end. True, the democratic process requires free and fair elections, but the ballot box does not necessarily lead to democracy. How so . . . ?"

The article was long and the analysis headache-inducing. Rahal did not waste his time reading it all. But his comment was ready. What were you saying, Abu Qatada? What were you saying? He remembered the heated discussion some days back, under Abu Qatada's virtual tent, on the Sharia ruling on elections. He borrowed Mahjoub Didi's avatar and email, and came up with:

"What democracy, what elections, what crap are you talking about, you secularist pedant? Elections that give all members of society equal voting rights: the believer and the atheist, the chaste veiled woman and the slut in tight pants, the scholar and the ignoramus. 'Say: are those who have knowledge equal to those who do not?' Besides, aren't elections an offence against the Lord of the Worlds? Lawmaking is the right of God alone and government is God's alone: 'Or have they associates who have laid down for them as religion that for which God gave not leave? For the evildoers there awaits a painful chastisement.'"

Champion your religion, Abu Qatada.

Rahal did not expect so many likes. More than fifty up to now, while the original article had no more than seven. The readers love your comment, you little Squirrel. True, Rahal did not agree with Abu Qatada's ideas. He wasn't an extremist who rejected democracy and elections in such an outrageous way. But the good reception given his comment filled him with zeal and pride. He had to find another subject to stick Abu Qatada's oar in. And God is the arbiter of success.

Translated from the novel *Hot Maroc* by Yassin Adnan,
published by Dar al-Ain, Cairo, 2016.
Longlisted for the 2017 International Prize for Arabic Fiction

IBRAHIM FARGHALI

The Temple of Silken Fingertips

THREE CHAPTERS FROM THE NOVEL, TRANSLATED BY JULIA IHNATOWICZ

The Temple of Silken Fingers (Ma'bad Anamel Al-Harir) is narrated by a manuscript which is abandoned at sea by its author. The manuscript relates what happens as it tries to reunite with its author, as well as revealing the author's past life in the UAE, Egypt and Germany. Weaved together with this are the adventures contained within the manuscript's pages: a story of copyists fleeing a city called the City of Injustice, which is dominated by extremists ruled by the head of a censorship bureau. On its journey, the manuscript is discovered by a number of new readers: the author's friend, pirates and an Ethiopian girl.

TOUT SAVOIR SUR LE VIN

Chapter 1

"In distant orbits, suspended in space, satellites are every hour taking pictures of our enchanting planet. To those who are ploughing through space, or to we who, courtesy of Google Earth, are looking at our computer screens it looks like a blue ball daubed in white, beautiful and peaceful. The giant lenses, every hour, are photographing, for those that want, whole countries, cities, or quarters, zooming right in on houses and buildings. Yet the satellites, despite their first-rate capacities, to this day cannot capture what is really happening on the surface of the Earth.

"They cannot observe what is happening there in the depths, in secret tunnels cleft through layers of the Earth's brittle crust. Some have been explored and charted, while others were until recently still unknown.

"I confess that I'm lucky, because I'm one of those forced by specific and complex circumstances – which will be described in due course – to seek out a distant refuge far out of reach. Thus, I found myself creeping through one of these dank, dark tunnels, crawling along, and at the end of the tunnel shone the light of my own realisation that I had fallen in with a bunch of fleeing scribes."

When the person who saved me finished reading these first lines on my pages, he closed the huge, blue, leather-bound notebook. Then he slipped me inside his leather jacket and made sure it was done up, such that I found myself confined to the tight space between his shirt and soft hairy belly, contemplating my fate.

He leapt from the floor of the wooden boat, where I had been discarded, to another slightly larger motorboat. After he had pulled the rip cord once or twice, the motor buzzed loudly and we set off.

In a while, the boat stopped and he shut down the motor so there was quiet all round. He disembarked by catching hold of the steps of a rusty old ladder and climbing up onto the deck of a ship.

He answered someone, saying: "No, I didn't find anything. The boat was totally empty."

A tumult erupted, cut through with shouting from more than one direction. I assumed the ship had fishermen aboard who had spotted a shoal of fish and started calling to one another. Their footsteps began to creak across the boat's wooden deck while they were running about. The man stayed still while the sound of feet gradually receded, eventually disappearing. Then he slowly began to move.

A short journey later – which I passed like a joey in the pouch of a kangaroo that was walking leisurely, no longer jumping, through one of the ship's inside corridors – and I heard the sound of a door opening and closing. As soon as the man pulled me out from inside his shirt, I could feel the moist beads of sweat from his body.

He opened my pages for a few moments, pondering over some lines at random, before closing me and putting me in a small drawer in the wooden bedside cabinet. Then he left the room.

And so I found myself alone again, suspended in the unknown. I recalled the scene of Rasheed's flight – he's the writer who created me from nothing – or to put it more precisely, his disappearance, for reasons partly unknown to me.

In the few hours just before he disappeared, he was worried, nervous and on edge. He took me out of a dark wooden drawer then pushed me between his things in a bag he carried over his shoulder. He threw this onto the bottom of a small boat that was secured by a thick rope tied to the steamer. Once he'd untied the knot, he sat in between the oars and started rowing vigorously, pressing on until we were far enough away from the ship for him to regain some of his composure.

Having recovered his calm, he opened the bag. He took me out to browse some of my pages and re-read them, until the sunlight faded. The easy monotonous movement of the boat, rocked by the little waves, soothed him, and thanks to the silence and the heat of the still air all around us he was overcome by sleepiness. Before nodding off, he put me down beside him. He opened the bag, took out a shirt, rolled it up and placed it under his head.

Before the darkness enveloped us, I was listening intently to the wailing of the wind and its whistle, which terrified me, not because of the screeching and howling, but because I have spent almost all my life confined by walls, stillness and silence. Then, all of a sudden, I was in the midst of furious waves, a hostage of the deep-sea storms, which seemed, to anyone who might see them, like the work of mermaids and the sea's other mysterious, mythical creatures. Stirring enraged from their deep slumbers, they transformed into waves that leapt and blazed with the daring of a lion, on legs of heaving water, able to raise gigantic battleships and turn them into playthings, all the while screaming wildly and savagely with a great roar of anger.

I felt the boat bouncing on the foaming waves as if it were going frantic. Rasheed woke and glanced around with a touch of fear. He got himself up and went towards the bow of the boat. Not a minute had passed before he was caught unaware and fell down beside me, tumbling onto the floor, moaning and clutching at his face, contracted in pain.

He rose to stand, and then I heard a rumbling sound coming from the bow. Someone sturdy and tall leapt in front of him and threw himself on him. Suddenly the man pulled himself upright and straight away fell on Rasheed again. He encircled his body, seizing him; he grabbed him by the front of his shirt with one hand while the other formed a fist and began punching him in the face. It was all Rasheed could do to try desperately to protect his face while the monstrous visitor abandoned all reason to the madness of his arms. He began striking any part of Rasheed's body he could get his hands on extremely violently while Rasheed lay crumpled on the floor. After that the dark-skinned giant straightened up and swapped his hands for feet as he embarked on a round of kicking.

The second the madman paused in his aggression and viciousness to contemplate his victim, I saw Rasheed lean towards the side of the boat and pull himself up onto his feet. Then with no prior warning or hesitation, he flung himself into the water. The giant's surprise at Rasheed's reaction lasted no more than a few moments before he too leapt into the water, and they both disappeared, leaving me alone.

For a minute or two I waited for Rasheed to return, but nothing changed, for hours. I was afraid, sprawled across the damp wooden floor, hopelessly miserable, abandoned beneath a sun that blazed in the sky and poured down its fires on me throughout the whole day before delivering me at night to the agents of darkness, cold and the stormy wind. I confided in the stars, glittering and glimmering from millions of light years away. But they weren't listening. Of course, they could neither see nor hear me. Nevertheless, with an eerie, persistent twinkle, they were sending me signals across the millions of light years, telling me to hold fast to the hope that they could catch my whispers.

I was bouncing about like a lunatic on the waves of the raging sea in that little boat, which almost capsized as the winds' fury and the waves both grew stronger.

However, with the strength of a miraculously saved drowning man, I gasped and my feelings shifted from black sadness and despair to a flood of elation when that handsome man I already mentioned arrived. He could not have been more different from the last one. I don't know how he came to me out on the open ocean to save me from my wretched, tragic fate, where the best I could have hoped for was to end up submerged in the depths, a feast for the seaweed.

Chapter 2

Tek tek tetek tek . . . Izzzzz. Tek tetek tek tek tek tek tek.

I really like the idea that I exist because of the strokes of a typewriter's metal keys on paper. However, my identity can also be manifest in other ways, like in the creak of a ballpoint pen or the dry rustle of a fountain pen's nib on paper.

You could say that I'm nothing but a voice, or more exactly a collection of voices, embodying an idea in the mind of a man who lived for a while in order to create me as I am today. Yet, I've been forced into silence; a silence that has seemed to me in hours gone by as if it would go on forever.

It's true that silence is a part of what I am and a part of my fate, but it is only one side of my nature. In this, my condition is like that of my peers. We spend most of our lives silent, obscure, shut on ourselves, watching and waiting for a hand to reach towards us, for fingertips to rest on our pages, to be open before the eyes of a reader, so that life can bellow inside us, so our voices can resound and resonate. We roar and revel in the characters and ideas floating in our depths. Our insides boil with the struggles of human souls, with the longings and wishes that flood over minds beset with anxiety, ruined human endeavours, and endless questions. We are taken up with other desires that watch themselves and claim to seek balance and completion. Together, these can represent part of humanity's voice, part of the soul of the universe, to which we must hearken. For we follow the paths of countries spreading across your world's continents, reaching expansive cities that glitter with lofty glass towers and modern buildings studded with the diamond lights of globalization; and we reach the dusty narrow paths and alleys of villages that are obscure by day and dark by night, silent but for the barking of dogs and the murmurings of fairies and night-time spirits, the creatures of myth and legend, unseen on your maps and unheard of except by those that live there.

My creator called me "the Taciturn", in the masculine form, but I don't mind. Even the greatest novels of chivalry had strange names, like Don Quixote de la Manche.

Ultimately, I can say that I'm nothing but a sunken novel, created on the open ocean after a failed attempt to write a biography and a few ideas, and maybe some stories and unfinished texts.

After a little while, I thought I would live and die here, without seeing dry land, where all the events contained on my pages happen.

My feelings of hopelessness were eased a little when I arrived on this ship in the hands of this handsome man, about whom I knew nothing. I feel that he must have a deep connection with my creator for this to have happened to me.

I exist entirely because of Rasheed al-Jawhari, a youthful man in his early forties. If you met him, you'd see a slim, handsome man. His face is chiseled, with kind, long-lashed, slightly hollow eyes beneath thick eyebrows. Usually, as was his way most of the time, he would be wearing faded jeans and a T-shirt of one colour or another. If one of you ran into him in the street, you would see an agile person, as exemplified by his walk that quickly propels his slim body forward, while he seems at the same time to be trying to slow his steps down, as if he were walking on tiptoe. Despite being well-built, he bends his neck forwards, as if bowing slightly; but he hides this with both his lean neck and his thick, black, curly hair which gleams with conditioner and looks like a dark halo around his head. Meanwhile, a quiet smile that has become his hallmark is etched on his face; to anyone who sees him, it gives the feeling that he is always at peace inside, as if he has fixed the smile to his face and then drifted off somewhere else.

As a teenager, his whole imagination was consumed by the dream of flying. He thought of it as a kind of miracle. Every trip with his parents, coming and going, to and from the Emirates, you'd see him sitting on the edge of his seat, joyfully watching the plane take off and land, as if these were two small miracles performed by a magician. He especially liked it when the plane's wheels touched down on the airport tarmac; when the giant metal bird, which only moments before had been hovering in defiance of the laws of gravity, laid aside its lightness in those bewitching seconds to reclaim its weight, bowing to gravity and surrendering to the pilot's authority. Thanks to this giant creature, the pilot is transformed, poised between two contradictory states, and trying, with a graceful touch, not to bump the plane's huge wheels on the runway. And here it evolves from a state of flying to whizzing along with a speed that surpasses any other vehicle, until gradually it slows, coming to a point of stillness and the end of flight announcement.

When this emotional transition between sky and earth was complete, at the moment when the plane landed and touched the ground – and even though the pilot's skill ensured that none of the other passengers felt this astonishing shift – he would insist on going up to the cockpit to shake the captain's hand and congratulate him on his remarkable talent.

He discovered in himself a passion for reading travel books, and one day he came across a copy of *National Geographic*. In it he read illustrated accounts of visits to a number of the world's cities, which were accompanied by high-quality pictures, shining on the magazine's glossy pages, showing peoples and places he dreamed of seeing and experiencing, body and soul. He was enamoured with the magazine and began looking for old editions, building up a colossal store of them that he never tired of studying and reading day after day.

The avenues of his mind expanded to the breadth of a single dream in which he saw himself as a traveller roaming all over the world. He would ponder the natures of humanity, abandoning himself to the lanes and alleys of different people's cities, uncovering their landmarks and thereby charting the soul of the people. He would observe their behaviour and feel out their customs and traditions, whether hidden or public. How did the layers of history pile up inside them to form their characters, which usually distinguish one people from another, whatever personal differences there may be between them? He would stay up with them in their nightly haunts and see what impression was left by their souls, thoughts, practices and particularities, what they ate, drank, and believed in to shape the soul of the city they inhabited.

He hadn't thought about it much before deciding to join the civil aviation institute, in the hope of becoming an aerial navigator. Initially, both his position in the middle class and his family (which was firmly wedded to the middle of this middle class – thanks to his father working for years in the Gulf and returning to work in real estate) enabled him to join an institute that had high tuition fees. This saved him from the only real alternative, which would have been joining the Air Force cadets. Fighting and military garb were not amongst his fantasies.

His father hoped to dissuade him from this dream and join a military college to become "a man", as he kept telling him, to learn some responsibility and acquire the necessary rigour to face life's difficulties, about which he could see his son still knew nothing. Rasheed, however, was set on his dream and stubborn in refusing his father's idea. He was ignorant of the aspect his judicious father hadn't mentioned: the cost of military studies was practically nothing in comparison with the huge burden of fees for a civilian education.

But he was prematurely schooled in calculating profits and loss – an act which knows nothing of ambitions, hopes or dreams. His father, who had experienced life's ups and downs, as well as its deceits, should perhaps have predicted what would happen. He went bankrupt, following a series of deals that left him open to being swindled by people he would in distress call "real estate Mafia sharks". Consequently, a year after he'd started, Rasheed, unwilling and miserable, had to stop studying at the institute. Inside he felt humiliated, dejected and a failure. A sum was paid to convert his credits at a humanities college to Cairo University, where he decided to study philosophy.

And so, the dream of entering the cockpit and sitting in the captain's seat to train, surrounded on all sides by a forest of electronic keys, was betrayed.

At first, he tried to do something so he could continue his studies in flying. He initially thought of working to cover the costs, as a trainee in a bar at one of the big hotels, as a waiter in a restaurant, as a business partner to a friend dealing in leather goods smuggled from Port Said. All of that, however, didn't even raise enough to cover a quarter of a year's tuition fees.

He went to two of his wealthy uncles to ask for a loan, but they both told on him to his father, whose temper flared. His father was overcome by disappointment and distress caused by his son. He had been trying so hard to keep anyone from finding out about his losses.

His father's anger was so extreme that he decided to cut all ties with his son. He would have done it, if not for the speed with which Rasheed's mother intervened in a death-defying attempt to persuade the "child of her heart", as she used to call him, to transfer to any other college for his studies and postpone his dream a little, until his father could regain his composure and deal with the grief of the losses he had suffered.

Rasheed considered the matter a personal failure. He buried his dream, so that he was then living in a state of total schizophrenia. He would spend time with his friends, like any normal person: smiling, laughing, playing football matches outside the University walls, or in various corners and lanes around Cairo, or on the open-air pitches of untouched neighbourhoods. Night and day – for he would stay up into the night with them every day. He would go with them as they roamed between the cafés in ancient Cairo's alleyways. But he did so distractedly, his mind occupied by a single question: "If I were in Paris right now . . ." Then he would be off on a trip into an extended daydream, during which he would smile absent-mindedly at whoever he was with. But if you had asked him what you were talking about, you wouldn't get an answer.

Daydreams pursued him from one airport to the next, from a landing strip in one country to hovering low over another airport. He was often able, at the edges of a film he was watching, to introduce a plane, or something conjured by his imagination, into the action, so that he could soar far from the film and its events into his own private world in a cockpit; he would face imaginary cyclones, feinting this way and that, challenging the perfidious storms and the wrath of the sky with its flashes of lightning and raging downpours; or, with cinematic skill, he would bring the plane down in an emergency landing.

Eventually, he was consumed by the feeling that his irrational life was at a dead-end. At the end of the day, it seemed an ongoing deviation from flying into the clouds of fantasy. He was forced to make a crash landing. Accordingly, he was open to hearing about the experience of one of his close friends, who was working as a sales representative for encyclopaedias and books with a marketing company. He considered the idea as a transitional phase between the imaginary and the real, then decided he would work in the same field. He signed up for a round of training. The person supervising the training of his group served as the real catalyst to his working in this area.

This man seemed extremely clever, modern in his demeanour and upright in his bearing. He had even features; wide black eyes full of intelligence, and heavy eyebrows that almost touched in the middle. He wore his thick black hair loose so it looked like a halo, making him more handsome; or rather it reinforced the charisma that was so plainly visible in his personality wherever he went. Likewise, he sported a trimmed, stylish beard and presented himself to the trainees as an affluent, modern man. It seemed that he leant heavily on this image in order to motivate them to knowingly give themselves up in a blood sacrifice for this work of selling encyclopaedias and leather-bound books. Sacrificing themselves to a dream in the hope of achieving what he had achieved.

Anyone who knew Rasheed before, as well as anyone who met him later, then described him as a chatty, self-confident, pedantic man. He told incessant stories of his continuing success in persuading people (some of them stars and celebrities in the arts) that they needed to purchase huge encyclopaedias on general knowledge, cinema, history, languages, science, engineering, and more.

He didn't tire of telling the other trainees and potential sales reps tales of his success. He managed to raise himself up from the first challenges of his youth, from a mere agent or rep, to a deputy for importing encyclopaedias, then a publisher and distributor. And he always relied on style.

Whenever Rasheed recalled that experience, he remembered what the man had said: "An idea can be said by a hundred different people in a hundred different ways, but maybe only three or four of those hundred people will be persuasive enough to get the ones they talk with to change their minds."

He explained to them that a deal would succeed whenever the rep was able to exploit his personal presence, his culture and charm in order to persuade whoever it was how much they needed an encyclopaedia or a collection of large leather-bound books to squeeze into their chic library, even if the rep knew that this was the very last thing that person needed. In the age of appearances, everything could be used for deception, everything was open to sales and commercialisation – even books!

When Rasheed al-Jawhiri first started recording his memoirs on one of my pages, he recalled memories of that time. He revealed that many trainees didn't grasp that charm and persuasion don't mean being chatty, or slimy, or a wise guy. This wasn't easy to explain and the ones that understood it easily already had the gift of persuasion. He would tell his trainees that each personality had its own special key, or a way-in that was linked to its own culture, social status and modus operandi. In his sardonic style, which he used to try and impress on them how likeable he was, he would add that the only failed rep was the one who thought it was simply a case of memorising a few phrases about the product he wanted to promote, and repeating them like a parrot.

As Rasheed laid down in writing, it was in this way, and thanks to Faisal Ameen – whose name he remembered for a long time – as well as his peers and ambitious trainees that "I filled the corners of the fancy houses built in the Eighties with massive libraries whose shelves were crammed with elegant volumes, forever closed and silent. Their owners were the nouveau riche who had created huge wealth in the age of *Infitah*, or openness, that characterised the Seventies. It had all come from currency trading and brokering, from trading in real estate and rotten food. For them, the concept of ownership was deeply and fundamentally rooted in a carnal lust for ostentation. They would show off anything, including large books stacked up in pretty wooden libraries between their salons and living rooms. There, they furnished their guests' eyes with a fantastical show that allowed them to claim membership of the elite. The nouveau riche considered culture a tool for social gradations within a class hierarchy that they had so insistently and odiously constructed. They envied it and used it to blot out the old image they had of their youth and childhood, replacing it with another that was more suited to their new gains."

Chapter 3

Does it surprise you that I know a lot about what goes on around me? Well, you have to understand that I'm a novel, which means I'm a depository of knowledge. But I have to adopt an artistic, literary style and form for this knowledge. I see with my literary senses. With my narrative insight, I perceive more than you see. I know what you might know, and sometimes what you don't know. My peers and I are alike in this: to start with, we submit ourselves to the minds and hands of our creators and producers. Then, once our main traits are in place, we jettison them completely and steer our own course. Even if we seem to you like taciturn, reticent, polite, static beings in the form of the books that you pick up and pass around, nevertheless we know that our essence is not the form in which you see us, between the covers of a book. Rather, we are tempests, which evolve from words into worlds of knowledge, ideas, fates and destinies.

Allow me to return you to the story of my creator, Rasheed al-Jawhari. I know the whole tale, even the bits that passed me by, as well as the bits that happened before he started writing it down himself. I know what he said to his friends and his lovers, with whom I coincided. I know about the sleepless nights when he would talk to himself like a lunatic. On some of those, he would drink glasses of arak until his soul was overrun by intoxication and he would scream like a madman, or he would use a little recorder to tape some thoughts for his novel – which I now embody. Or he would take pleasure in talking about himself, and address himself in soliloquy, recalling his biography in his masculine, slightly nasal voice. Meanwhile, I would be sitting nearby, heeding all he was saying with all of my senses, although I definitely didn't know that I would be forced to recollect his story in this way.

Let me tell you about Rasheed, from what he once explicitly recalled and recorded in front of me. He was amazed by the character of Faisal Ameen, the trainer for selling books and encyclopaedias; by his manners and the intelligence he enjoyed; by the verbal vitality he would use to convince clients to buy a solid cultural product. He did this despite knowing full well that the wealth of the product, embodied in collections of sleek volumes, would go no further than a fixed spot on a library shelf where it would be surrounded by other books, packed in to make a pretty picture for the library owner's pleasure. Their contents, however, meant nothing to the owner. The likes of him cared nothing for the volumes except in so far as they allowed him to be called "cultured" by any of his ilk, those who frequented his house as friends and acquaintances, and those with mutual interests: the slaves to wealth and formalities, the environs of the bourgeoisie, in a life built entirely on superficial appearances.

In this experience of embarking passionately on his working life, and in others later, Rasheed's certainty met with no doubt that he would travel some day and commence a journey continuing long enough for him to traverse the world. This certainty, however, was not able to conquer the feeling of bitterness and distress that had taken possession of his soul.

He realised then that his dream of being a pilot was a seminal part of his dream to tour the world. This wasn't just because he was madly obsessed with flying a plane, soaring through the skies around the world. It was also part of suppressing a deeper idea, the core of which was a passionate love for the idea of moving through time, or more precisely, the idea of a lightness that could defy gravity, as when a giant jumbo jet weighing several tons seemed no more than a feather, drifting between the clouds. This was why he had a serious fascination with car racing and films depicting the adventures and manoeuvres of war planes.

Perhaps that's why he chose that strange dream for this novel's hero, where he drives a truck along a highway that exists nowhere but in Rasheed al-Jawhari's imagination. It may also be that in that scene he was expressing his personal frustration.

The door to the room opened and I listened. My saviour came in and closed the door. He came towards the drawer where he'd put me and picked me up with both hands, contemplating my cover, a blank page with one word on it: "Taciturn". Then he headed for the little bed in one corner of the narrow room.

I considered him, with my powers of perception, for the first time. He seemed to me athletic and physically strong, with handsome features and large eyes that looked upon the world with an intelligent gaze. He had neglected to shave his beard or moustache for several days. His hair was long, black and thick, braided into a plait hanging down the back of his neck and sprinkled with many white hairs.

He threw himself onto the bed exhausted and gazed distractedly at the ceiling. After a few minutes, he picked me up and sat up straight. He opened one of my pages to pick up where he had left off:

> "I recalled her in a dream. She came to me, blaring and bursting with energy, in red as dazzling as a meteor and massive as a mythical giant. Whenever she came near, she showed me how much savage beauty she had. Her roar echoed all around as my own nervousness mixed with a dormant feeling

of excitement that all but ruptured my soul. The truck of my dreams. She was colossal and had a spacious cabin. Magnificent and gleaming red, she towered high, with no trailer. She stood proud and haughty as a lion on her ten tyres.

I mounted the silver metal steps that were covered in tough little bolts and breathed in the smell of the leather covering the adjoining comfy black seats. I gazed at the driver's seat that looked more as if it belonged in the cockpit of a plane than in a truck's cabin. There were speedometers and rev counters and shining panels in different colours for the different bits of equipment. The gear stick was topped by a round black grip of compressed plastic that shone prettily.

I found myself excitedly driving her along a highway that twisted and snaked its way, thrusting between a bottomless ravine on the left-hand side of the road and a rugged mountain on the other. The mountain was orange, mixed with stretches of light brown and yellow, and over its sides were scattered little bushes whose green leaves had turned pale with the mountain dust and scorching sun.

I clung to the steering wheel that turned at the touch of my insignificant hand; right and left, according to the bends of the road. I was trying to rein in a strange feeling of unjustifiable dread. While driving at top speed, according to what my eyes gleaned from a stolen glance at the speedometer, and with my focus sharp on the road, I knew, with a mysterious, prescient sense, that in a moment's time I would discover that the truck's brakes didn't work. And I would keep hurtling forwards with the inertia until I perished, unable to stop the truck, clutching the steering wheel as if it held the secret of life, determined to hang on for some miracle to stop the vehicle before it tumbled into the deep ravine.

I got past the gust of loathsome fear that had struck me to the core when I saw a girl on the side of the road, whose attractive form suggested from afar that she was a pleasant creature. She was standing by the road and waving at me. I hesitated for a few seconds. I was afraid that the moment I decided to stop for her would be the fateful moment when I would discover the brakes had packed in. But I put my foot on the brake pedal and the truck slowed down. I took a deep breath and gradually stopped. I found the girl's face peering in through the cabin window after she'd taken hold of the door. I indicated that she should get in, while I looked at her smiling face, the beauty of which reminded me of the Mexican actress Salma Hayek. A woman's perfume, mixed with a faint smell of sweat, flooded over me and its fragrance quickly spread. All the while, I was staring at her gorgeous eyes and my attention was captured by a pin-prick of a mole on the end of her little nose.

As soon as she sat beside me in the cabin, I started driving again. The conversation between us was weird. She spoke a language I didn't understand at all and what I said also seemed to make no sense to her. Nevertheless, we kept up our strange conversation. Meanwhile, I turned from time to time to look at her attractive, supple thighs with the sun's rays reflected on them, or her breasts that were straying out of her black T-shirt.

The amazing thing is that we kept on talking in words and various gestures. Our conversation was uninterrupted save for her occasional bursts of giggles. Eventually, I stopped the truck after we saw a bar by the roadside with buses and lorries crowded in front of it and groups of guys and girls standing around laughing together, smoking, and knocking back small dark bottles of beer. We passed them as we hurried towards the bar. We were both excited by a level of happiness for which, at least for me, there was no excuse save the presence of this lovely girl. She moved with a childish vitality and had a permanent smile drawn across her enchanting features. The smile seemed a fixed trait and didn't change except for contractions of her pretty little face, when the smile was quickly transformed into peals of laughter.

We sauntered in through a narrow glass door and came upon a great multitude. They were spread out in clusters around circular and rectangular wooden tables, enveloped in smoke and a tumult of raucous laughter. We found only two girls there, standing by the bar whispering to each other like a pair of lovers.

The lights were dim. Their faint red and blue glow reflected off the tables and the indistinct forms of the people around us. The Mexican girl drew my attention to the bar's wooden ceiling with glee and excitement. I looked at where she was pointing and laughed. The ceiling was covered in women's panties in different colours and styles, hanging at random next to bras in a range of colours.

A handsome old man approached us. The loss of his hair did nothing to detract from his good looks, which were enhanced by a thick moustache. What was left of his hair was white. His face was a bloody red and his shaven skin glowed in the light. He was sturdily built, wearing a green cotton shirt and jeans. He pointed to the ceiling and asked how far we were prepared to adapt to the house rules. Comprehension dawned on our faces. He explained that only men came into the bar and women were not allowed in without a registration of this kind, and he pointed to the ceiling.

My friend asked him how come the two lover-girls were there. He chuckled: 'They're not wearing underwear either.' She laughed shamelessly and without hesitating put her hands under the short denim skirt she was wearing and swiftly wriggled to remove a pair of blank panties from beneath her feet, one after the other. Then she presented them to the man with a shy smile. He snatched them up gratefully and rubbed them into his nose, saying in a both friendly and crude way that her smell was good. She smiled flirtatiously. Meanwhile, my confusion had turned into a dim-witted grin that I proffered them both while I was imagining the little hairs around her vagina that had given the panties the fragrance he described as 'good'.

He asked us where we would choose to sit so he could put the panties above it. She pointed to a distant corner next to a window overlooking the road.

I saw her sit down exposed in front of me, with her pitch-black hair hanging down over her shoulders. Her breasts lay easy on her chest and she leant her arms on the table. She was talking but I was captivated by her eyes and didn't hear anything she said. Or, I was gazing at her lips, which moved energetically. I stole glances at the panties and bras hanging over our heads, fascinated by the vitality of her ever-smiling face, by the halo of black curly hair cascading over her bare shoulders, by the enigmatic smell that occasionally wafted around us.

She was looking at me coquettishly. I smiled and then whispered: 'Your body is very lovely.'

The scene was interrupted by the appearance of a group of naked girls, standing and looking at us. I noticed a resemblance between one of them and a cousin of mine, so I moved towards her smiling, but was surprised by a huge man approaching the girl I had been sitting with and kissing her. She got up, with a wide grin on her face. Then the details that came to me from the dream grew confused and muddled, until I found myself alone, driving the truck again at almost top speed and clutching the steering wheel in the hope that another car wouldn't come towards me. While I realised that I was dreaming, I could not rein in either the nightmare or the truck, which seemed like a devil that had commandeered my fate. I lost control of the vehicle in the end, as it resisted me and swerved off the road. I told myself again and again that I was dreaming, dreaming, and I would wake up now. I screamed like someone appealing to be woken from a dream that doesn't want to end. Then my soul suddenly went into a black bubble and I couldn't feel anything at all.

* * *

I woke annoyed, hating the dream and myself. As I have a poor memory for them, I have lived almost entirely without dreams. But now, I am alive only in my dreams, or rather in my nightmares."

There came a sound of faint knocking at the door to the room. My saviour bolted upright. He hid me beneath the pillow then stood up, went towards the door, and opened it.

Excerpted from *Ma'bad Anamel Al-Harir,*
published by Difaf Publishing and Editions El-Ikhtilef,
Beirut and Algiers, 2015.
Longlisted for the 2016 International Prize for Arabic Fiction

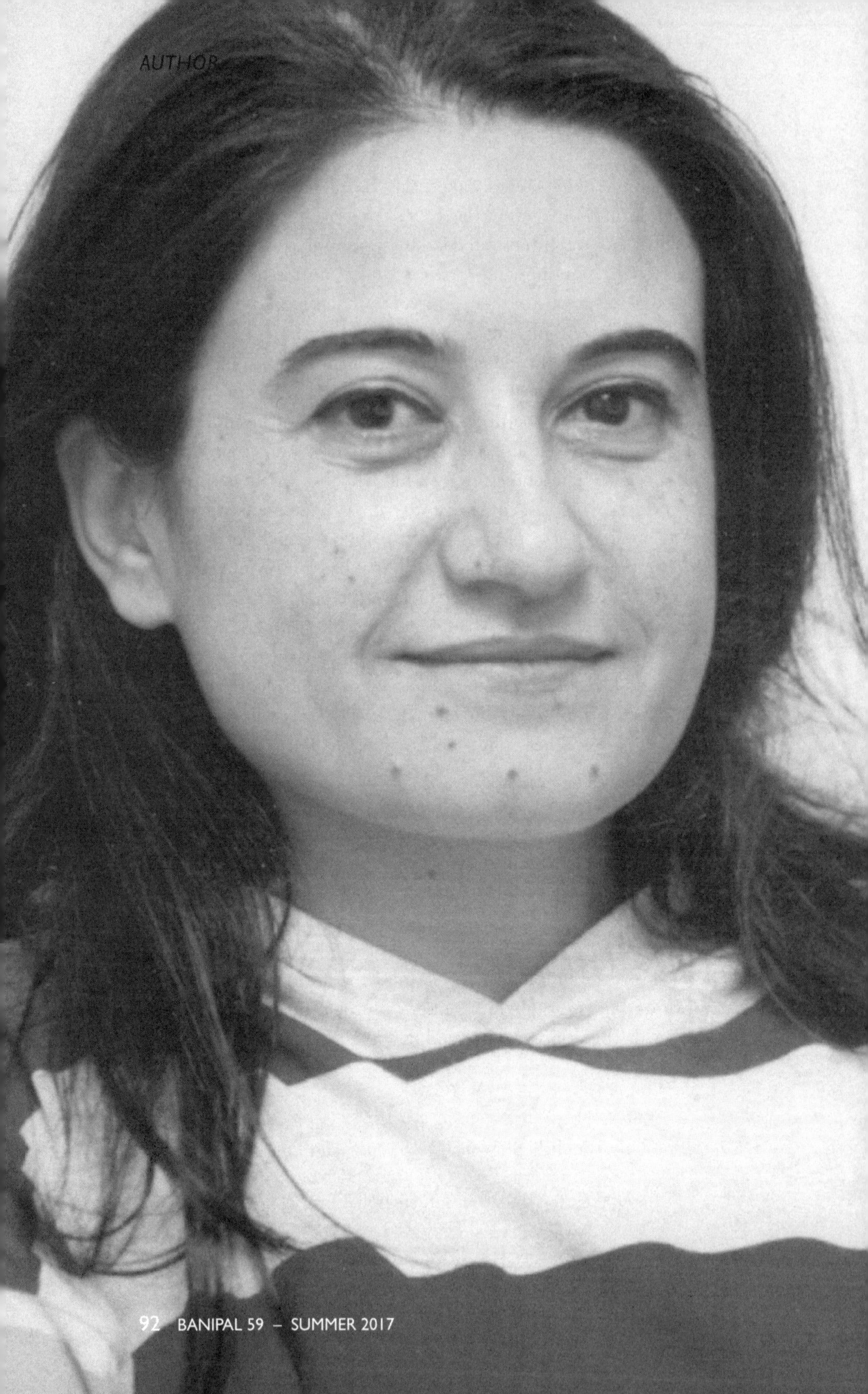

RENÉE HAYEK

The Year of the Radio

EXCERPT FROM THE NOVEL,
TRANSLATED GHENWA HAYEK

I left the hospital on January the 15th. A deep red scar snaked up my arm. My mother wrapped her arm around my shoulder and held on to the dangling left-hand sleeve of my jacket. My father walked ahead of us to the car. As soon as she was sitting down inside, my mother asks him about the hospital bill. He replies "Later."

Before we arrive home, the rain had started. A Sukleen truck was collecting the garbage. The traffic stopped. My mother turned around to talk to me, and asked me if I was in pain. For what felt like the tenth time, she began to list all the people who had called, and all those who had visited me while I had been in my brief coma. I could have pretended to have amnesia, and treat them all like complete strangers to get a bit of rest. In the days of my recovery, I heard my parents repeat the story of the accident to my friends and relatives. Each time, they bowed their heads and said: "Thank God. May He show mercy to Samer's parents." Then, they would assure their audience that I had not known him before that night.

That part was true. I had not known him. I got into his car to give Chrystelle and Ahmad some privacy. Ahmad had invited Samer so that he could introduce us to each other. I smoked one cigarette after the other that night. I answered some of his questions, and pretended I couldn't hear others. I learned more about him from the things I heard after the accident. I don't really remember how it happened. I had my earphones on so that I wouldn't have to make small talk. Samer had reconciled himself to that after several failed attempts to get me to remove them. He had met a girl at the club, and had danced with her for the latter part of the night. I remember the girl more than I remember Samer. She was eighteen at most, wearing a short, cropped shirt that exposed a colourful dragon tattoo on her waist. The tattoo caught my eye because its colours were deep and shiny. I try to recall what he was wearing, what colour his eyes were, but the only thing I remember were his slender, soft fingers and his discomfort with cigarettes. He kept saying: "Isn't smoking banned in closed places?"

I stare out the window and try to recall the accident. I fail. Why can't I recollect the details? The only thing still in my memory is the sound of the violent crash. I don't even remember that I hid my head in my arms.

The taste of the medication leaves me constantly nauseated. I look at my father's head, at the white hair and permanent stoop of his shoulders. It's not the white hair that makes him look old – after all, my mother dyes her hair, and doesn't look any younger. They were old even when I was a child. All of my friends' parents are younger than mine. I remember how, in 5th grade, I befriended Dima just because, like me, she had old parents. But Dima was an only child and got everything she dreamed of. She was the first person in our class to get a mobile phone; she got one before she even knew how to use it.

The cigarette I light does not raise any complaints; all my parents do is open the windows. It lets the drizzle in. I know they won't say what they usually do. Did I not just miraculously survive? My mother says that to every single person who calls. She repeated it to my sister

The Year of the Radio by Renée Hayek is set in contemporary Beirut. It is the story of a young woman working on a limited contract as a school speech therapist. At the end of the school year, her contract is terminated and she tries different things before finding a job for a year at a radio station. There she works as a psychologist, presenting live programmes in which she offers advice to the parents of children with speech and psychological problems. Over the course of a year, we follow her experiences of love, loss, work, illness and unemployment.

Rita, who, unusually for her, had been calling every day. I envied Rita, who was fourteen years older than me. She had left right after graduating from nursing school. Her departure for France had been unexpected, but she is free now. She has her work in the St. Jean Hospital near Lyons, and lives with her boyfriend. When he visited Lebanon with her two years ago, my mother told all our relatives and acquaintances that they were engaged. My father avoided speaking to Pierre. I often heard him arguing about my sister and her boyfriend with my mother in the early mornings. My mother chafed at his constant nagging, and would ask him: "What can I do? She's your daughter as much as she is mine. She's become French, and behaves like they do." Then, she would add, as if trying to remind him: "She's been far away for eighteen years, and independent, and now you want to teach her manners?" I used to laugh at that, but then she'd glare angrily at me until I left the kitchen. My sister Clauda is the only one of my siblings to have my parents' approval. She was a brilliant student. She studied pharmacology, married a pharmacist, and has two lovely children. My parents boast about their grandchildren's impeccable upbringing, Clauda's intelligence, and her husband's manners. To rankle them, I don't use her name, and I don't describe her as my sister. Instead, I say things to them like: "Your daughter called." When she got married, I was not then even ten years old. Despite that, I fought with her every time she visited. She always had something to say about my grades, my clothes, my friends. I would tell her: "You're neither my mother nor my father." One of those two would then rush to tell me to shut my mouth and respect my sister. Eventually, I got used to going to my room every time she visited and I was at home. Sometimes, I would tell her I felt sorry for her children for having a mother like her. That was the harshest thing she could hear. Her tears would flow, and my mother would call me a stupid good-for-nothing.

I feel lost without my phone. It shattered in the accident. Whenever my mind drags me towards Samer, I tell myself that I didn't know him, so why is it that I feel so sad, and why do my thoughts stubbornly return to those forgotten moments? Who was he? I didn't even learn his family name or what he did until after his death. My parents want me to sue the driver of the car who caused the accident. I asked them what a lawsuit would do. I don't know why I feel as responsible for causing his death as that insane motorist who was driving the wrong way. The image of him in my mind is the one that was distributed following his death. My mother would show it to visitors and loudly bemoan his lost youth. I don't know where she got the picture. Perhaps one of my friends had given it to her?

I was surprised that so many people visited me at the hospital. I hadn't seen some of them in years. I think they were curious. People are drawn to tragedy. George didn't call, my mum said, but she found excuses for him. "They may not hear news from Lebanon in Dubai," she said. The next day, she was less charitable: "My sister in Canada heard the news. So why hasn't he called?" My mother had been really upset when we broke up; we'd been together since our school days.

I can see the seven stitches over my right eyebrow clearly, despite the smudged car window. The doctor said that, in time, the red colour would fade, and I would be left with a thin white scar. The shards of glass had also cut my neck in several places. The doctor said that had one of them been a few millimetres off, it would have caused a lot more damage. My mother repeated that phrase to my visitors, and embellished it by adding that the injury would have sliced my neck off.

Two young boys run between the cars at the red light. One of them, the disabled one, approaches my mother. Unusually for her, she gives him 1,000 liras. She generally berates me for giving the younger kids money, saying that it's taken from them and doesn't help them at all.

As we reach the beginning of Hamra Street, my father starts losing his patience. Even after all these years, he still hasn't got used to the traffic on the way home. Before his retirement, he took a taxi to work. I was the only one in the house to drive the old Mercedes. People turn to stare at us in that car, because it's so unusual. "It runs perfectly, so why would I buy a new one?" is his response every time I complained that it's hard to steer, or that its manual transmission is tricky, or the windows don't work. I eventually stopped complaining, and had even begun to grow fond of the car, especially since it's so different. I used to drive it to work during the two years I was working, and take it on long drives. During my studies, my father wouldn't let me drive it to Achrafieh. At the time, I took the bus or a service taxi, up until I met Chrystelle. She owned a large Jeep, and would let me drive it. She was a clumsy driver and was no good at parking it. She didn't even have a good sense of its dimensions. I remember our trips to Byblos, with the music cranked up and bottles of wine going back and forth. I often felt that I was the happiest one among them, even though I never drank as much as they did. I could drive like that for hours. I loved the smell of the salty, humid air, especially at the start of winter. We sat cramped in the seats, seven or eight of us. Even though most of them had their own cars, we preferred to ride together. Her car smelled like those trips. Neither time nor multiple washes could change that. As soon as the car door opened, out wafted the smell of cigarettes, and hashish, and perfume mingling with the scent of our relentless, unflappable energy.

The traffic light turns from red to green several times, but our progress is inch by inch. My mother scolds him for not taking the sea route.

I feel sleepy. The sedatives keep me in a semi-comatose state. I may have fallen asleep, because my mother had to shake me awake when we finally arrived.

The humidity inside our house keeps it as cold as a cave. My mother rushes to the phone, saying something indecipherable about callers. In my bedroom, I spot a small sofa and two chairs. When I turn to my mother inquisitively, she says they're for visitors. The worst thing about this whole thing is that I have to stay in bed. When I try to look at the computer, I get exhausted before I can even finish

Hamra Street, Beirut

checking my emails.

I pretend to sleep. My mother exits slowly, shutting the door behind her. The presence of people around me has irritated me. I wanted to sleep, but I can't. I try to listen to music, hoping it will help quell the images crowding my mind.

She had placed paper clippings on my bedspread. I had asked her what they were, and she told me she had gathered them from the newspapers. She didn't know why all the papers had our family name wrong. She was upset that they had called me Yara Ghazali, instead of Ghazal. I read a one-sentence description of the accident in the security bulletin roundup. In the obituaries pages, there were eulogies for Samer from his school's alumni association, and from Byblos Bank, in addition to those by his family. I asked my mother, "What do you want me to do with these?", and pushed them off the bed and onto the floor. She picked them up angrily, and called me ungrateful. She had not slept a wink while I was in hospital, and had just prayed and cried. Even at school, they had felt more sorry for her than I did. I had covered my head in the blankets, and she left the room, grumbling.

The din of the angry car horns blaring outside blends with the clatter of pans in the kitchen, the whir of electric drills, and the smell of boiling chicken. Since his retirement, my father has taken to doing repair jobs in the house. My mother's dislike of the mess he makes while working was one additional trigger for their arguments. He painted the walls twice in one year. He made a shoe cupboard that my mother refused to use because it wobbled. Like many other things, it had ended up either on the kitchen balcony or the garbage dump. My mother tried to encourage him to leave the house, to no avail. She then assigned him the task of buying things for the house. That had been her job until she argued with the butcher and the grocer. When she was instructed by her doctor to start walking along the seaside Corniche, he started joining her, no matter the weather. Rain or shine, they got up, put on their waterproof jackets, and left the house before the sun rose. Sometimes, he took a second walk during the day. My favourite thing was when the house was empty. With the years, I've become increasingly irritated by my parents. I don't know if it's because they changed, or whether they had always been like this, but I was finally seeing them properly.

When she called me, Chrystelle told me that Ahmad was not doing well. She had gone with him and a few of Samer's friends and relatives to a candlelight vigil at the site of the accident. She told me I could see the pictures on Facebook. I asked my mother to tell those who called asking for me that I was asleep. I didn't want to talk to anyone.

If I had been in less pain, I would have left the house. The food my mother put on my desk got cold. I didn't touch it. The hot steam filled the room with the smell of chicken soup. The smell brought back a specific memory of my dad's mother. She was a quiet woman. We made fun of her country accent. When my dad brought her to live with us after my grandfather died, she fell ill and began talking incessantly. She told stories about her parents, about her childhood toys and the French soldiers and her brother who had died. She forgot we were her grandchildren. My parents argued and argued, until finally my father agreed to place her in an elderly care home in Roumieh. The only time that I went to see her, with my dad, she had recovered her memory, somewhat. She knew who we were, at least. They brought in her lunch: chicken soup, with pasta shells floating in it. She would not taste it. My father asked her how she was, and she said she was well. Then she fell silent until we stood up to leave and she said: "Son, take me with you, please, I beg of you." We sat back down, and my father tried to calm her down, and explain that here she was receiving the medical care she needed. She replied, "Son, what am I doing here?", and told us of people coming in at night to beat her and tie her up. My father looked at me, and said, as if to himself: "Your grandmother is a bit confused." Then my grandmother picked up her rosary beads and began to mutter as if we were not in the room. The woman she shared the room with, who had been sleeping, sat up suddenly in bed, then crashed back down onto it with a loud shriek. Teeth floated in a glass on the nightstand near her. My grandfather's handkerchief with its embroidered white roses that he used to put in his blazer pocket was also there. I stared at it so that I didn't have to look at the bowl in front of her and cry. It smelled of urine and medicine and mould. I wanted to run away from there and never return. She asked us to feed her chickens and water her plants. My father said: "What chickens, and what plants are you talking about, Mother?" She made a face, and told him to turn off the lights because she wanted to sleep. It was bright daylight outside. We both looked up at the unlit ceiling lamp, then left. On our way back, my father did not say a word. He didn't even complain as he usually did about the heat, the traffic, or the crazy driving conditions.

That was the last time either of us saw her.

* * *

The coffee I'm drinking has been cold for at least an hour. When I lift my arm, the sleeve shifts and I can see the beginnings of the scar. I don't think it's getting any lighter, despite what the doctor said. It seems to be turning black, in fact. My other scars are healing faster. The thing that annoys me the most is that everyone who sees them asks me how I got them. The crowd starts to thin around me, only the old people discussing politics and reading the papers remain. A few students from AUB are around too. Their chatting distracts me from my book. I don't think I'm making any progress. None of its words stick in my mind. I look at the pictures hanging on the walls. Each time, I notice a new detail I hadn't seen before.

I rarely run into anyone I know in here. All of my friends are either at work, or, like Chrystelle, who went back to study business management, back at university studying for graduate degrees. She wasn't in any hurry to find a job. She enjoys university life. Her father advised her to study business, arguing that her psychology degree wouldn't get her very far. My speech pathology degree didn't get me very far either. Neither did my master's degree, which I had paid for by working for two years. My mother said I was stupid for losing my job. She said anyone who worked in a school should keep their mouth shut during their probationary period. I don't think I did anything wrong. I was hired as a speech therapist, not knowing that I would be expected to accompany students on their field trips and be a surrogate teacher whenever anyone was absent. I objected when it all became too much. I was working a full day with no break. Although the principal had agreed to let me leave at noon twice a week so that I could attend my lectures, he would always plead extenuating circumstances that required my presence whenever I tried to go. In the beginning, he tried to flatter me, saying that I needed to observe the young children in their natural environment. Over the two-year period I worked there, I visited every soap factory and olive oil press, every historical landmark and orphanage in the country. I even went to a woman's prison with the senior class. Once I'd received my MA,

I asked for a meeting, and requested that he formally set out my job responsibilities just as he had done with my colleagues, so that I would be in charge only of following up speech disorders and attention problems, as well as other psychological issues. During our conversation, he said that education was not a job, it was a vocation, and many other inanities. Even so, when I received a termination notice at the end of that year, I was shocked. I searched in vain for another school, but they had either already filled my position, or did not offer those services. Some of my classmates worked in doctors' clinics or psychologists' offices, but I didn't know anyone who could help me get my foot in the door for that kind of work. In my class, we had been mostly women, with the exception of one male student, Talal, who left the country to begin his doctoral studies immediately following our graduation. Many of my classmates had married and were raising children.

All of my plans vanished in a puff of smoke. I couldn't go backwards and ask my parents for money. I took on any temp jobs on offer, no matter how humiliating I found them. I enjoyed private tutoring the most. My mother found me a few students from the school where she worked, and one student led to another. Their parents were eager to hire me because they thought I was a therapist. They expected me to work miracles on their children. In the beginning, I tried to correct their assumptions, but then I stopped. I teach two students regularly, and am paid two hundred dollars a month per student. Before that, I worked in retail. The semi-illiterate manager would ration our bathroom breaks, and forbade speaking during work shifts, which were over eleven hours long. We were only allowed to sit if we were in pain or ill. Our lunch break was fifteen minutes. I was so desperate when I took that job. The most mortifying thing about it was when one of my classmates from school or uni came into the shop. And all of this humiliation only brought in 400,000 LL a month ($250). I lasted two months in that job, but it felt like two years.

Excerpted from *Sanat el-Radio* (The Year of the Radio),
published by Dar Al-Tanweer, Beirut, Tunis and Cairo 2015.
Longlisted for the 2017 International Prize for Arabic Fiction

ZUHEIR AL-HITI

Days of Dust

EXCERPT FROM THE NOVEL,
TRANSLATED BY SAMIRA KAWAR

Father Fraidon, the pastor who officiated at the "Holy Family" church in Baghdad and tended it, entered my life like the blade of a sharp knife, slicing it into two equal parts: a before, and an after in which I had become different.

At the time, I was still a university student in my last year. His footsteps had begun to be heard throughout the neighbourhood in which we lived. His exciting arrival and assumption of his sacred duties caused an unusual stir. Stories and gossip about him spread quickly: his firmness, and his ability to attract worshippers to the church, which before his arrival had been almost empty except for a few old people. But there it was, usually full of people during most mass services, and overflowing on Sundays and religious occasions. People even started to speak of miracles that he performed here and there. The popular imagination, full of half-truths and myths, turned him from an ordinary pastor into a popular one. Unlike his predecessors, he no longer only spoke to them of hellfire and seduction by the devil. He used to focus on love, mercy and tolerance. His reputation spread beyond the Christians to the Muslims who lived in the neighbourhood. Everyone was talking about him, and when they did, they would drop their voices and hold their hands in front of their mouths for fear of saying something unworthy of him, or that infringed upon the halo of his popularity. People are drawn to the sacred, but they also fear it.

The story began when Mary, the cook who had worked for us since the days of my grandfather, the Pasha, asked my mother to relieve her of her tasks because she was old and wanted to return to her place of birth in the north. Her three sons had emigrated and settled abroad, two of them in America and the youngest in Australia.

Mary had a nice house close to our mansion. I knew it well, because as children we used to accompany her at times to play with her sons, Touma, Maher and Nameer. It was made up of two storeys, and in its midst was an open-air eastern-style courtyard. In the midst of that was a disused, dried-out fountain, but Mary had turned it into a beautiful spot by planting various flowers and plants that gave off a pleasant scent. I was very taken by the design of that charming Baghdadi house, which seemed to me to have just jumped out of a mythical tale. After reading the fairy tale of the prince and the frog, I started to enjoy sitting near the fountain, waiting for the ugly frog that would climb out of it and turn into a good-looking prince before my eyes, taking me to the heart of the myth.

After the death of Younis, Mary's husband, who had worked for us overseeing maintenance and repairs, Mary lost hope that her sons would return. So she decided to return to the village of Bartala, where she had been born, to die there, since she no longer had any motive to remain in the city that had witnessed her youth, the birth of her children, their departure and the death of Younis.

The beautiful house had started to suffocate her with its memories, both sweet and bitter, as she put it. Nostalgia beckoned her to return to her roots, to that faraway village, asleep for thousands of years on the Nineveh Plain. She knew that she would eventually be buried in the family cemetery near Younis, and when she described it, her eyes would brim with tears and longing. It was situated on a hill outside the village, and her ancestors and Christian history reposed there.

Days of Dust is set after the fall of Saddam Hussein and the invasion of American occupying forces, when Iraq descended into chaos. With acts of murder committed in an attempt to purify the country of its former regime, mobs sow fear in the hearts of people across Iraqi society, most notably within the Christian community. Ghusn al-Ban's family had built its fortune and reputation in the days of the monarchy. Using her relationships with various Christians and the great art collection of her grandfather, Ghusn al-Ban follows the transformation of Iraqi society in this novel.

Mary rejected her three sons' repeated invitations to join them and settle with them in their strange new world, which frightened her. The most she wished for was to see her sons before departing and dying in her village, so that she could then be buried on that hill and become part of the long Christian story in the Land of the Two Rivers. Mary had only two regrets about leaving: the first was parting with my mother, whom she loved. The second was parting with Father Fraidon, the new pastor, "who restored a love for the church amongst parishioners in the neighbourhood, which has become well-known in recent years for its excessive promiscuity," according to Mary. She added, "He's not like the other pastors before him, who used to encourage the young to emigrate abroad, to be swallowed up by absence for ever" as had happened with her sons. "On the contrary, Father Faidoun is against emigration."That had made him very popular with her and many other Christian mothers, who were unable to leave the land that they had inhabited and loved, and were consumed with grief at the departure of their sons to such faraway, or cold places. Mary used to refer to him as though she were talking about a saint who had just jumped out of the Bible, and was walking and living amongst us in the Bataween neighbourhood.

All that and other talk that I had heard about him peaked my curiosity. It seemed to me as though she were talking about the mysterious prince for whom I had long waited at the edge of the dried-out fountain in her garden. I had awaited his appearance so that he would ask me to kiss him, liberating him from the curse placed on him by an evil witch, and then taking me away with him to where I knew not.

When it was time for her to bid me farewell, she drew close to me with a hesitance that she overcame with difficulty, then opened her arms and embraced me. I smelt between her neck and the edge of her hair that was pulled back into a black scarf the scent of a history threatened with extinction! I reacted with the same affectionate feelings she was showing. I was unable to stick to the family instructions of rejecting mixing between classes, a value we had preserved for generations. This was dear Mary! I embraced her and expressed my genuine affection for her.

She said: "I don't know when I will die, but I hope that I will not be apart from Younis for long. You know that I rejected the idea of selling the house despite the many tempting offers I received, even though my sons agreed to sell. But I refused and told them I would remain in the hope that those who were absent would return. If any of them returns, he will find a home awaiting him. They all know how I love you. I have informed them that I will leave the key to the house with you."

She pulled out a key ring to which two keys were attached: one to the front gate, and the other to the house. I did not hide my joy at being tasked with this duty. Her house was dear to me as well, and full of beautiful and precious memories. I promised that I would visit it once a week, and that I would water the plants and trees she had planted until God's will was done.

Mary's tale drew my attention to something I had not paid attention to before. The arrival of someone with the status of Father Fraidon in the neighbourhood, which had become shared, was not a very important event to us Muslims. But it was very important to the others! Before his arrival, we had never heard a Christian voice amongst us. They had lived as though they were in a "ghetto". We could hear them speaking the Syriac language, and preserving it as though it was what gave them their identity; and they always met everyone with friendly smiles. Things started to change some time after Father Fraidon's arrival, and we began to hear sounds of celebration. Before then, that "ghetto" had been an invisible world to me, although many of them worked for us. Their world was quietly established without noise when the city was established, if not before, and they carefully avoided anything that could provoke the Muslim majority because they realised that patience and circumspection were the best way to preserve the Christian presence, that stretched back before Islam, from melting into that tumult that no longer accepted diversity.

Father Fraidon, who adhered to Christian values, was of the view that protecting the Christian presence in Iraq depended on being part of society rather than being segregated from it. The Christian values in which he believed were human values that were not exclusive to one category of people. As for faith, it was an individual issue between a believer and what he believed in. Adopting those values was the way to protect Christians in that vibrant neighbourhood, where mixing between the religions was familiar, and where the borders between the two religions were so narrow that they sometimes became blurred.

Since his words about the common human spirit spread, his name was on every tongue. Even Mamloukah became obsessed with Father Fraidon, and started bringing news of him to us, or rather to my mother, who had a particular weakness for anything supernatural and sacred. The news of him that she brought mixed fact with myth. Rumours spread that he could perform miracles, was a messenger of virtue and was stern with deviants, that he inspected small houses and dark corners in bars in search of those who had despaired of salvation, that he bestowed blessings upon everyone until he got to know them one by one. He did not differentiate between Christians and Muslims, and spoke to everyone. Respect mingled with fear, producing a sacred mix, and he was undoubtedly a representative of a divine authority in the Bataween neighbourhood. During the era of the monarchy, the neighbourhood had been one of the grandest in the capital and had been inhabited by well-known families. But as time went on, it turned into a commercial district that included several of the most famous hotels frequented by people coming from distant and nearby regions, because it was close to the capital's medical centre on Nasr Street. The clinics and offices of the best-known doctors and lawyers were situated on that street, as well as real estate bureaus and the offices of import and export firms and international airlines. Moreover, it was close to the jolly heart of Baghdad, known as Abu Nuwas Street, which stretched all along the banks of the Tigris river and was home to bars, restaurants, fun fairs and brothels.

The large number of prostitutes and pimps living in the Bataween neighbourhood to be close to their places of work was the biggest threat facing the neighbourhood. So Father Fraidon focused his work on that contrary aspect. None of his predecessors had managed to make the kind of headway that he achieved. The priest roamed all parts of the neighbourhood with confident steps day and night. At first, the parishioners he was visiting met him with cold indifference because he had come to change their habits and way of life. But the coldness gradually turned to acceptance, and then to affection, and ended up as something close to sacred veneration.

One cold foggy morning in January, I left the mansion and headed for the university but with some hesitation as there was no real reason for me to go there that day. I just wanted to get out of the house rather than stay in the mansion all day. The road was almost empty, except for him. I had never seen him before. Perhaps he was going to tend to a dying woman, to read her some passages he had chosen from the Bible, helping her to overcome her fears and move peacefully into the other world. Our eyes met, and he inclined his head towards me with a gentle smile that I later learned never left his face.

I do not know why I was confused and unable to return his greeting, despite his warm smile that flowed over me. The man was very handsome and attractive, and his face seemed like a nature beauty spot that beckoned one to a stroll! He looked exactly opposite to my preconceived image of him. I did not doubt for a moment that he was the famous priest. Even the neighbourhood Muslims had grown to know and respect him, because the need for miracles is not confined to one religion. In my confusion, it was difficult for me to determine his age, but he seemed to be in his late thirties. He was wearing a black robe with a white collar, the way Catholic priests do, and a scarf around his neck with religious symbols all over it. A rather large wooden cross hung around his neck, and he was not wearing a cap on his head. In his right hand was a Bible that he carried close to his heart. He was tall, rather thickset and of an athletic build. He had a short beard slightly infiltrated by white, and it matched his short haircut.

He quickly passed me by, leaving behind a lingering whiff of a strange perfume mingled with the scent of church incense, and a mysterious, inexplicable trace of something, before being swallowed up by the thick fog. Up till that moment, I had been searching for my sexual identity, which had been unclear because I had repressed it until I could find the right person. I had long been hearing an urgent call emanating from my body, but I had been unable to recognise or define it. In that flash of a moment, it seemed to me as though my body was leading me in spite of myself. It was the eternal call that emanates from women's bodies since the dawn of creation, prompting them to rebel against their minds, which always tried to control them.

To be sure, I tried, at the beginning, to repress that call, which surprised me with desires that were out of step with the traditions and customs with which we had been raised at the mansion, and which were transformed into the incontrovertible fact that we were different to others.

The fate of Julnar, whose name had never been mentioned at our mansion after her departure and her erasure from our lives forever, frightened me to death. I wanted to remain true to the traditions that I had believed in as a life choice, but I felt that my resolve had been shaken. I don't know why seeing him reminded me of the sin, and why Julnar's image became associated with that of Father Fraidon!

The conundrum snowballed in my mind, despite my attempts to ward it off. It was difficult for me to ignore or forget it. Now, I don't know if I had really wanted to at the time, or not!

The pastor became a very strong presence at the very heart of my life. I used to listen out for news of him from the servants and peasants who worked for us. I had not until then been interested in keeping company with the women who got together in my mother's kitchen in the late morning to have coffee, read their fortunes and exchange news and secrets. But following that foggy morning that had left me dizzy, I could not get his image out of my head. To my mother's astonishment, I started to attend those late morning sessions in the hope that they would mention him in their chatter. Although this usually happened, it was not enough to quench my thirst for him. News of him was always mixed in with exaggeration and tales that I could not possibly believe. This bothered me, and I would think of forgetting him. But I could not.

I hesitated very much, and was very frightened of my weakness, but in the end, I decided to visit the "Holy Family" church where he worked, living in the adjoining house. I did not think of justifications for this strange visit, but headed for the church as though I were unconscious and unaware of where my destiny was leading me!

I had visited the church before on a few occasions, but I realised that my visit to it this time was completely different. I went to the spot where votive candles were lit by those making vows and special pleas, lit a candle, placed it at the feet of the Lady of Sorrows and made an obscene wish.

The church was empty, except for a pathetically thin young woman, wearing black from top to toe. A black, embroidered shawl was aesthetically draped over her head. She was kneeling in front of the first row of seats, and very close to the figure of Christ crucified upon the cross. She was speaking to Him in a low voice that she slightly raised at times, but her words remained unclear and only intelligible to the two of them. She did not look straight at him, but held her head slightly turned to the side, either out of respect or fear, I could not make out which.

Her hands were clasped in front of her bosom, and a rosary with agate beads and a golden cross at the end of it dangled from them. The girl seemed as though she wanted to catch a shadow or a soul, or maybe she was searching for hope.

Not far from her, a rather plump lady flitted about like a bee as she carried out her daily cleaning chores, her gaze shifting between me and the girl wrapped in black. Perhaps she feared the girl would melt and vanish out of piety before Christ bleeding on the cross. After she saw me lighting a candle to the Virgin, she stopped moving around and started to look straight towards me with a boldness tinged with some caution. She definitely knew everyone who came to the church. I felt slightly disconcerted, because the last thing I wanted was to speak with someone I did not know. So I remained standing before the Virgin's statue, not quite knowing what I was doing there.

The soothing cool and gentle dimness seduced me into sitting not far from the thin girl, and to enjoy that strange calmness that insulated me from the disturbing chaos on the surrounding streets. I began to study the walls of the church, which were full of primitive paintings that betrayed amateurishness and their creators' lack of talent. But the religious awe that their chosen subjects inspired was moving. The artists had chosen to focus on the sad hour of the crucifixion as it was related in the Bible. It seemed to me that combining the Bible account of it with painting prompted the observer to sympathise with the paintings, irrespective of their artistic value, which had not been the artist's main concern. But because I had studied art, I could not ignore their primitiveness, which bewildered and troubled me. The church was dark, even though the sun shone brightly outside. It also had a slight musty smell that mingled with Omani incense . . . and the smell of a man I had come in search of.

The pale light that seeped into the middle of the church through its dusty windows spread an atmosphere of sadness that stuck to the body. It seemed as though the plump lady had not cleaned the windows in a long time. The old wooden pews were dark brown, but the parts of them on which people sat had turned to light brown, as though every believer who sat on them had come away with a bit of their colour, leaving an indelible trace. How many people had sat hear listening to the sermons and speeches of priests, harbouring their fears, wishes, boredom or piety, desires for a divine miracle and their sins which they had brought here in the hope of finding salvation. And many other things.

I sensed all this, and that feeling gave me a strange enjoyment, and my heart told me that my visit would not be the last.

I repeatedly visited the church when it was empty of worshippers. It was normal that a kind of friendly relationship should spring up between me and the plump cleaning lady. Once I introduced myself and she heard my family name, her look of suspicion disappeared. I learned from her that the husband of the thin girl who always wore black had emigrated to Denmark three years earlier, and she had not had any word from him. She used to come and pray every day, to beg that his fate had not been the same as many young immigrants, whose dreams had been buried at sea.

My visits to the church were motivated by a wish resembling that of a mischievous jinni living deep within me, dancing with incredible daintiness, tickling me and promising me a meeting with him, despite my guilt, which would not allow me to easily act on my madness. His shadow had remained with me since that foggy day, and pushed me towards recklessness and an abandonment of all the ideas I had been brought up with, which were in stark contradiction with my foolhardy impulse.

What was the secret behind it? Was it the myths that were spun around him and spread through the street of Bataween, or within its half-darkened apartments, its bars, its miserable corners and the mansions of the rich?

Had his handsome looks dazzled me as I beheld the most beautiful of Baghdad mornings in his face? In fact, it was not important to me to know why I wanted to see him. What mattered was that I did. Chasing his shadow had begun to bring me happiness, pleasure and an addiction to something I had not known before. More importantly, I had shaken off the boredom that had dominated my life at the time.

Excerpted from *Ayam el-Turab* (Days of Dust),
published by Dar Al-Tanweer, Beirut, Tunis & Cairo, 2016.
Longlisted for the 2017 International Prize for Arabic Fiction

ABDELKARIM JOUAITI

The Moroccans

TWO CHAPTERS FROM THE NOVEL,
TRANSLATED BY MBAREK SRYFI

The Militarization of Blindness

You may call this chapter "Militarizing of Blindness" or "The Blindness of Life". Months after the death of my grandfather, my older brother returned from the war in the Moroccan Sahara wrapped in a traditional burnoose, concealing his eyes behind dark sunglasses, and leaning on a cane, dragging his right leg because he had had a knee replacement. He returned with a face scarred by land mine shrapnel; he looked as though he had had smallpox. Like most maimed soldiers returning home from battlefields, he was distracted and silent, unable to believe he was still alive. He was transported to Marrakech Hospital and from there to the military hospital in Rabat, where he underwent operations with team after team of doctors and nurses, his prescriptions were changed, and various medical analyses and X-rays were repeated. New pieces of shrapnel, which had been missed in previous examinations, were discovered, and he drifted from one coma to another, from sharp to excruciating pain. He was visited by the Angel of Death, who for some unknown reason refrained from taking his soul; his body failed him when he was on the verge of jumping from a window forty metres high in the first hospital; and in the second hospital his medication was taken away after a nurse caught him trying to gulp down a cocktail of anxiety pills.

Since then, precautionary measures were put in place when he was moved from one hospital to another, after a note warning of his suicidal tendencies was added to the end of most of his medical reports, but these precautions were unnecessary because he'd had a strange

spiritual experience that allowed him to be at peace with what had happened to him, or at least allowed him to slowly, calmly and patiently swallow the bitterness of his handicap.

After his return home, my brother would divide up his time between caring for me – endeavouring to protect me from the affliction of blindness – and writing a flow of complaints and requests to the General Command HQ as well as open letters to newspapers to demand compensation for his violated rights. He would return home glorious every time he dropped a letter in the post box. But doubt, despair and disappointment would quickly dissipate his fleeting hope. He would doubt that the letter reached its destination, which would push him to write more copies of the same letter and put them in different post boxes. Sometimes he would question the style of the letter and as soon as he'd dropped it in the post box, he would doubt the style of the letter or he would convince himself that a word in the letter was inappropriate, or that a sentence did not make a totally crushing argument, or that there was a problem in the structure. Then he would rewrite the letter with earnest, noble and impassioned ardour.

He was chasing a meaning where all the shadows of pain and injustice that befell him intensified; he would experience a temporary and ephemeral happiness at carving an amazing sentence, which would show its betrayal of what irritated the soul. He began to go to the market and buy books: diaries, short stories, and novels, as well as books on how to write letters, and he started to use citations and borrow words and expressions from them to prevail upon hard hearts unmoved by any wind. An unintended side effect of the magic

The Moroccans follows the central character, Mohammed al-Ghafaqi and his relationships with his grandfather, the Pasha, his military brother and the neighbours' servant girl whom he loves. It tells of how he is struck by blindness and of the broker who betrays him and steals his wife. Interwoven with this central narrative are the stories of the grandfather, the graveyard of skulls and other tales interlinked with political and social resonance.

of literature, however, was that it thrust him into a despairing sadness. No matter how he tried, he could not succeed in utilising the power, influence, and accuracy of the writers. He would leave one book for another, go from one letter to another, anxious and sad, smile coldly at us, then turn his back on us, and stretch out, contemplating the ceiling and the waves of thoughts crashing about inside him.

He told me something many months later: books of fiction are full of pain and tears, but they never reach a single moment of real pain. The greatness of literature resides in its total uselessness; it is a wild flower growing beside a road where angry elephants cross. Then, for some reason, he suddenly stopped writing letters, and he quit waiting. I was puzzled by that but did not dare ask him why. Maybe reading literature had opened his eyes on the rudeness of the world and filled him with despair at the impossibility of amending its injustices and abuses. From the very first days of his return, he seemed unable to reconcile his soul with the future of long unemployment thrust upon him, to accept the destiny of his body, which would not permit him to do anything; maybe that's why he considered it his mission to save me from my coming blindness. He took me to the doctor in the clinic many times, undertook putting my eye drops in himself, followed up on the effects of the medicine, and he visited my school to ask about my grades. He would implore teachers to pay special attention to me because I was threatened by a disease, advised me to sit in the front row and stare at the board. You don't have enough time, he would say and would constantly repeat: "Stare." I would stare and stare, and the letters and figures would appear to me swaying, drunk, and the lines delirious. I remember my estrangement and my sensible but bewildering silence, my loneliness, hesitation, trembling, my constantly watery eyes, and my intense need for a moment, one single moment with my grandfather in the field. I never knew how I passed all my classes every year, nor how certain things found their way deep inside me: snippets from chants and poems, images ripe with longing for cheerful birds, dancing butterflies, and flowers that never died – while other things passed me by like dark clouds. I remember when I ran after the neighbourhood children as they were chasing a puppy, and how they sneaked through barbed wire while I got caught on it and the barbs stuck in my chest in a long bloody hug. My wild scream of pain as they tore into my blood still resonates inside me. I remember my repeated falling into streams and holes that my peers had easily conquered because I had misjudged distances. And my ever-erratic handwriting, my sleepless nights, my dreams of golden palaces, green rivers, merciful female genies, and fig and pomegranate trees. But I don't remember how I ended up with glasses strapped round my ears, the lenses thickening year after year, or how the magic of the *halqa*, the storyteller's circle of listeners, in the nearby souk took a hold of me. As soon as the school bell rang in the evening, I rushed to join the convoys of affliction and destruction, and severe calamities, and Sayf ibn Dhi Yazan leaving the island of monsters, or on his way to Egypt to bring the Book of the Nile from the city of Qaymar[1], or watch Barnukh the magician fighting other magicians, casting on them the spell of tremor. But they would reverse it, casting on him the spell of awe, which he in turn would reverse, casting on them the spell of cardiac failure. He took from them and gave to them, and they took from him and gave him back . . . I would run to meet the childhood of the world, where children don't die, are not defeated, where the marvellous walk, where people are transformed into crows, monkeys, pigs, and rocks. And courage is sufficient to subdue evil forces, and open preserved treasures, and win protected lovers . . .

After my brother despaired of the clinic's doctor, he took me one morning to a Romanian eye doctor call Bazov, who had opened a private practice in the administrative neighbourhood. We did not know what wind led him here. He was short and fat, spoke a funny Arabic, examined you with his eyes – which were small, deep and piercing – and would hold you with a hand as dry as a gravedigger's. He checked me over extensively, then picked up a sheet of paper and explained my illness to my brother in a neutral way, with the coldness of a torturer. And with a distressing flourish, and without caring much for what he was going to say about my small tender heart, he drew a circle and told him: "This is a lake." And he drew many lines going off it like sunrays and said: "And these are tributaries that feed it." Then he asked: "What will happen if these tributaries dry out?" My brother slowly replied, bitterly dropping the paper, having comprehended the ugliness of such pedagogy of loss: "The lake will dry out." Bazov looked happy with his intelligent answer and added: "The boy suffers from high blood pressure in the small veins linking the eye to the brain, and such pressure will cause gradual damage and eventually retinal vein occlusion. And after a few years he will face the fact of losing his sight."

My brother's features became tense, and he said softly, as if whispering to himself: "What now?" Bazov answered with deadly severity: "Nothing . . . prayer and supplication." As we were about to leave his office full of sadness, he added arrogantly, fixing his gaze on my brother's cane as if to avoid giving us any impression of being rude and cruel: "This world and its civilization is created by the sick, handicapped, and crazy; the strong have only created wars." My brother pulled me fiercely by the hand, compensating for his fury at not having had a chance to demolish the evil Bazov, and he departed, shaking from anger and disgust, cursing him. But starting from dawn next day, he began a literal application of Bazov's advice: prayer and supplication. He woke me, jabbing me violently and ordered me to perform the ablution, and after I prayed behind him, he took out a book called *Dalail al-Khayrat*[2] and began to read eagerly, with me repeating after him in deceitful diligence for I did not know what I was repeating. I wished he would hasten his reading so I could go back to bed, yet I could not understand how the reading of supplication would deter the hand of fate from crashing down on me. This early morning torture lasted for months, I learned *Dalail al-Khayrat* by heart, and a few Suras of the Qur'an, and some supplications that would melt rocks, making them offer delightful water and milk and dates. But the benefits my brother and I were hoping for, that of my cure or at least a delay of my date with blindness, never came. My brother was lost for words by an intense sadness when he checked my eyes and noticed they were getting worse and worse; and like a raging bull he began to renounce all the devotion, fear of God, chants and invocations we had cultivated for months and that had given us hope. After a long silence, he said to me, citing someone whose name I don't remember: "Belief has not succeeded in moving real mountains from their places, even if some claim that, but he knows how to put mountains where there aren't any." Then he asked for forgiveness and went out.

The following dawn, he woke me up as usual, we prayed and I returned to bed; he called me to recite from *Dalail al-Khayrat*, but I didn't answer and he did not insist. I heard his cane strike the ground as he walked away, and that was the sign of the end of the epic of my failed spiritual cure. For more than a month he kept his distance. He did not talk to me, he would avoid even looking at me, and when we get together at home, he would raise up the book he was reading as if to put up an immune wall of paper between me and him. Did I fail him to that extent?

The Return of the Dead

Their heads could barely be seen in the large ditch they had been digging for days; they were happy because they were not suffering the same difficulty as at the beginning, but slowly defeating the rocky, hard, compacted red soil. And here was this same stubborn land, after their patient work, rewarding them with its first line of defence collapsing, revealing moist and crumbly black soil requiring no pickaxe. They found rocks, bits of iron and plastic, and, as they went deeper, the roots of two huge trees, which the construction project had required to be cut down.

They were two of the willow trees the French had planted beside every water course in the city to create shady places for evening walks, and after Independence people had nothing else to do but chop them down. Since the morning, the diggers had been arguing about these roots, and whether they would die with the mother tree, or stay alive, and given suitable conditions, would a new tree grow.

They went down about three metres when one of them struck something and gave a soft screech; he struck again and uncovered pieces of something white; he bent down, picked one up and examined it, then showed it to the others beside him, and they all agreed that it was a piece of bone. He bent down once more and uncovered a human skull. On the side of the ditch a digger discovered another whole skull, and within an hour, the diggers had six skulls in their hands. Apart from the first one, which had been broken by the pickaxe, they were all intact except for a few fragments.

The men all climbed out of the ditch terrified, but prepared tea, sat down to smoke some kif and sip the tea, while wondering calmly what to do. One of them noted the strangeness of finding only skulls without the rest of the skeletons. They were all astonished: should they tell the authorities? Or should they bury the skulls and continue their work as if nothing had happened, for all God's land hides wonders? If they informed the authorities, work might stop, and the contractor, who had hired them for seven days – and they had only one more day before payday – might find an excuse to avoid paying them. And if they returned to their work, as if nothing had happened, would the authorities, who had eyes everywhere – even on the pickaxes – would they be punished for treating the skulls as if they were bottle caps?

Whose heads are these? When were they buried? Are there more skulls?

They smoked for a long time, drank tea, argued, discovered other unanswered questions, their voices slowly rising. To put an end to their endless arguing, one of them withdrew to a place they used to go to the toilet, and from there sneaked out to the street, and later returned in a police car.

Such a secret could not remain secret for long. The news spread rapidly in this bored city that for months had been craving such news, a city where nothing had ever happened until these six skulls decided, with their strange return, to provide a topic worthy of analysis, interpretation, imagination and terror.

I walked with everyone to the place. The police had barricaded the area and were keeping curious people like me away. Police officials of every rank were milling around, smoking and talking on their cell phones. There were also journalists poking their noses in the ditch, taking pictures of the six skulls. Nothing happened for two days. People would go about their business and pass by the place, trying to divine information from the source. The barricade was the same, so were the fearful officials, who carried on milling around, smoking and talking on their cell phones.

On the third day, a decision was made somewhere, and the workers were back digging, under the supervision of the officials, and every few minutes a new skull would appear in the hands of one of the diggers and, after being registered with a number on a label that hung from the jaw, it was placed next to the others. Another decision came, informing the diggers not to follow the line of the ditch, but to dig in all directions. And, like the original ditch, these new ones were full of skulls. A pile of skulls was formed, a pile so high that no one could agree on their number. Some said there were a hundred, others said over two hundred, and others said there were even more.

The mass of piled-up skulls was increasing every day, and so did our estimations. The diggers extended beyond the construction site, getting closer to Tamagnout Avenue. I was one of the daily faithful to the show of skulls, one of the active people in the great discussion waged by the bystanders about the identity of the dead, and about the mystery of the skulls without bodies. I suffered, like most people of the city, from nightmares, where skulls came from the vault of the earth, with shocking stupor and voids for their eyes and empty mouths. I thought at first, it must be a crime, but when the number of skulls grew I said to myself it must be a massacre. When the pile grew, I said it must be a genocide, and when the skulls formed a mound, I said it must be a violent war or a small Armageddon.

One morning, the bystanders exchanged copies of an article from a national newspaper entitled "Discovery of Historical Cemetery in Beni Mellal". The writer, as it turned out, did not know anything more than we did, the only addition worth mentioning being the confusion of the authorities in dealing with a strange cemetery. No one knew its origin or significance. Hence, the authorities' continual milling around, smoking and talking on their cell phones, did not reflect any control of the situation.

Ibn Tumart[3] arrived and he disturbed our show, circling around us repeating: "Aren't you ashamed, you bastards, watching the bones of ancestors being treated like dogs' remains? Long live the King. Long live the Holy places. I spit on you . . . spit on you all." Ibn Tumart debated with the entire city mercilessly every day, delivering speeches in front of cafés in fluent Arabic. Whenever he sees a group of people, he acts as if he were commissioned to propagate virtue and prevent vice, warning people of the affliction and diseases he himself is holding back lest they befall the city. He brandishes some amulet or talisman he had made to scare them. He speaks some gibberish, as he loves to do, without forgetting to always add: "Long live the King. Long live the Holy places."

Years ago he had been sentenced to two years in prison for insulting the King and the Holy places, and, due to his undisputed insanity, served every day of his sentence. Afterwards, his lunacy manifested itself in a despotism more powerful than his previous delirium, for in his jabbering he never forgot to repeat the refrain of "Long live the King. Long live the Holy places", no matter what the topic of his ranting was, no matter how his agitation increased, no matter how

Beni Mellal, Morocco. Photo by Samuel Shimon

much he foamed at the mouth.

Just as the authorities always handled anything disturbing that had no instant solution, they set up a big official tent, where they hid the excavated skulls, and fenced off the digging site with huge tin boards, so our curiosity could not be satisfied any more. They did the same thing with the poor side of town, so why not with the dead and strange skulls, which had shown up from the darkness of history to disturb their peace and quiet? Despite that, we kept going back, gathering around the strange cemetery, and exchanging news until we came up with the idea that someone could climb up the big tree nearby, and from there everything could be seen, even inside the big tent. We learned that the number of skulls had massively increased, that the diggers were getting closer to the street – two metres from it – and that the officials were still milling around, smoking and talking on their cell phones. And again, Ibn Tumart showed up, tall as a bamboo in his white clothes and cane – the only things he ever owned. He was angry and stormy as usual, shouting frantically: "You bastards, can't you see that the earth discharges its burdens? Pray, fast, give alms, and cleanse yourself, ye citizens of Beni Mellal. Long live the King. Long live all that's sacred . . . Spit on you . . . Spit . . . I spit on you all." And he went off, threatening and cursing. I followed him and remembered that time when a soldier and I saw him pestering customers in a café, calling on them to go to the mosque instead of staring insolently at women passing by.

I had smiled and the soldier squeezed my hand, saying: "History is a big game of backgammon. If Ibn Tumart, this clown with his sharp tongue and knowledge of jurisprudence, finds, like the original Ibn Tumart, a group of followers who dignify and admire him like Abd al-Mu'min al-Kumi[4], Muhammad al-Bashir al-Wansharisi, or Abi Hafs al-Hantai . . . if he finds a sultan who restrains himself from bloodshed like Yusuf Ibn Tashfin[5] . . . and a negligence of time and people crushed by the harshness of life, who inevitably turn to religion . . . and if he finds inaccessible elevations like the mountain of Tinmal that would give him time and shelter to ripen and strengthen his mission . . . he will have a great position. In this country, small details and cunning chances can make you either an inspiring leader or a senile madman." He and I had continued walking, and after a long silence, as I was pondering over what he'd said, he then added: "Unfortunately, history only records the crazy people who have succeeded in becoming leaders. As for those who crushed their heads against the rocks of reality, there is no mention of them."

The authorities leaked some news that they had summoned a special committee from Rabat to investigate the strange cemetery, to date the skulls, and decide what to do with them. One day, after people circulated the news of the committee, the authorities stopped the digging, because they were tired of what the earth was discharging. Days later, the enigmatic chemistry of a skilful hand succeeded in turning people's attention to the scandal of a faqih caught red-handed in a mosque having sex with the muezzin of the same mosque.

Our people have short memories, and their interest in issues is fleeting. That is why they quickly forgot the cemetery, washed their hands of it, and turned their attentions to the muezzin's arse.

And yet here I am with a few people who frequently visit the place of the skulls, waiting for the honorable committee. We are unconcerned with our faqihs, with their caprices and excessive virility, who offer, from time to time, scandals to a thirsty public, and to an authority, trying to buy time, terrified that the people may unite around what is beneficial to them . . .

Excerpted from *Al-Maghariba* (The Moroccans), published by al-Markaz al-Thaqafi al-Arabi, Casablanca & Beirut, 2016. Longlisted for the 2017 International Prize for Arabic Fiction

Notes:

1 The medieval epic adventure tales of Sayf ibn Dhi Yazan are based on the life of Sayf ibn Dhi Yazan, a king of Yemen of the 6th century CE who triumphed over invasions to his kingdom. The stories combine fantasy, fable, mythology and Islamic ideals into popular tales retold orally through the ages.

2 The *Dalail al-Khayrat*, the Waymarks of Benefits, is a compilation by 15th-century Moroccan Sufi scholar Muhammad ibn Sulaiman al-Jazuli (d. 1465) of litanies of peace and blessings upon the Prophet Muhammad, otherwise known as "the guide to benevolent deeds".

3 Ibn Tumart (Berber: Amghar ibn Tumert, ca. 1080–1130 or 1128) was a Muslim Berber religious scholar, teacher and political leader from southern Morocco. He founded and served as the spiritual leader of the Almohad movement, a puritanical reform movement launched among the Masmuda Berbers of the Atlas Mountains. Ibn Tumart launched an open revolt against the ruling Almoravids during the 1120s. After his death his followers, the Almohads, went on to conquer much of North Africa and Spain. Source: Wikipedia

4 Abd al-Mu'min al-Kumi (1094–1163), called by Ibn Tumart "the lamp of the Almohads", took over from Ibn Tumart after his death, extending his power over all northern Africa as far as Egypt and becoming the first Caliph of the Almohad empire in 1147. Muhammad al-Bashir al-Wansharisi was one of Ibn Tumart's first followers.

5 Yusuf Ibn Tashfin (d. 1106) was the Berber leader of the Moroccan Almoravid empire of western

SULTAN AL AMEEMI

One Room is Not Enough

CHAPTERS FROM THE NOVEL,
TRANSLATED BY JOHN PEATE

Prologue

In a small room, in an unknown place, someone is peeping through a keyhole at someone peeping through a keyhole at someone else in the room next door. They are all spying on other people endlessly, and that's all they are doing.

Chapter 1

In a room that isn't mine, one I don't recognize, I wake from sleep surprised to find myself alone. I look to my right and see a black telephone on a small, drawerless side table next to the double bed with the blue bedspread that I'm lying on. I sit up. There's a plain, grey book next to the phone, with no picture or design on the front. It's entitled *Sole Choices*. The author's name is my own.

I don't recognise this book. Never heard of it. How can I – someone who has never attempted more than a few short stories that I'm too embarrassed to publish – find my name inscribed on a book as the author? How?

I daren't open the pages. A voice inside me says: "Ignore it. Keep away from it." There's a switch on the wall above the bedside table. I flick it and the room is plunged into pitch-black. I flick it again and there's light once more from the neon bulb in the ceiling's centre.

Photo by Samuel Shimon

The walls are grey: my favourite colour. It makes me feel tremendously calm inside and brings peace to my soul. And, even though it's winter, the temperature in the room is reasonable. There's a picture on the wall opposite of a black cap with a tie below it of the same colour, though it's decorated with red crows, some of which hover away from the tie, turning black.

I remember my mobile phone. Where is it? It must be in my pocket. I feel for it, but can't find it in the strange one-piece nightgown I'm wearing. There's a single pocket on its left, which has a dried-out red biro inside it. Surprised to find it there, I take it out and put it near the book. I pick up the phone. There's a continuous dial tone. I try and call my mobile, but the line goes dead as soon as I dial the third digit. It could be a hotel-style phone, so I dial nine, like you do to get an outside line, but it immediately goes dead. I press zero to get through to the operator, but nothing happens. I put the phone back down.

I wonder where my mobile is, and where I am, and when I came here, and who brought me. What had I been doing to end up in this place?

I try and remember. Then I do remember. I'd been walking at midnight in one of the side roads behind the hotel where I was taking my annual holiday. Then . . . no, I can't remember what happened next. I concentrate. I close my eyes. I try and remember, but my memory betrays me. I try and work out what might have happened

One Room Is Not Enough sees the hero of the novel wake alone in a strange room. He doesn't know how he got there and there is no way out. Through the keyhole of the door, he discovers someone else is living a normal life in the adjoining room. This person looks like him, behaves like him and has the same hobbies, but he is unable to communicate with him. In the room he finds a book entitled *Sole Choices*, with his name on the cover as the author. It contains a strange introduction, but the remaining pages are blank. In an attempt to escape his isolation, he fills the blank pages with the peculiar history of his family, followed by the account of his experiences in the room and what he sees as he spies upon his neighbour through the keyhole.

to me. Have I had a bang on the head, been knocked out and brought here, like you see happen in films? I feel my scalp. No trace. Have I blacked out for some other reason, and someone has brought me here? Have I been given an injection? I don't know!

OK, I must stand up, get up. I feel such weariness in my limbs, like I've just played a lot of sport after a long break. I get up. The floor's really cold. I look at my bare feet. I can't see my shoes anywhere. I go to the door to the right of the bed and try the handle, but it's locked. Fear engulfs me.

I notice the door has a keyhole you can look through. It's one of those that takes a big, old, jagged-toothed key. I haven't seen one like that for years, maybe not since we moved out of the old house. What's behind the door? I bend down to look through the keyhole to find out. There's another room, with a man standing in it putting a book on a bookshelf that looks like mine. Then he turns around so that his face is straight in my eye line, and sits down. I look closely at him. That man is me.

Chapter 2

That "me" is wearing the pyjamas I normally wear when I'm travelling. He's sitting in front of a TV screen watching a foreign film starring Meryl Streep. I always follow the movies of this star, but this film seems strange, I haven't seen it before. I guess it is a new one, because in her face I can see she is not young any more. He doesn't notice me turning the door handle. Maybe it's because he's preoccupied with something. I call my name out to him while looking through the keyhole, but he never turns around. I shout louder: "Excuse me!" He doesn't stir. The TV isn't loud. The sound is certainly low enough to hear my voice. I try and open the door again. I jerk at the door handle, but my double doesn't move an inch. It's like he can't hear anything. Impossible for him to be hard of hearing, because he's watching TV.

I need to calm down. I go back and sit on the side of the bed. My eyes take a tour of the room. Beneath the picture of the crows there's a medium-sized fridge. I walk over and open it. It's full of ring-pull cans, bottles of water, cartons of good quality juice, and easy-peel fruit you don't need a knife for. There is enough food to last someone a week.

I think of a knife! Of course! If I can find one it might somehow help me escape. Maybe to break open the lock, or dig a hole in the wall to make my escape. I've seen it done in so many films. There's an open door to my left that leads to a small bathroom. I go in and look around. There's a handle only on the inside. The bathroom's very small. Just a sink and a toilet. There's no extractor fan in here. It'll stink. There's no mirror, either, and no towel. It'd be hard to have a wash in here, and impossible to see your own face, to reassure yourself how you look. I exit the bathroom and go back to sit on the bed. What am I going to do here, I say to myself? And what is my double next door going to do? Maybe I'm dreaming. I must be dreaming.

Drowsiness still lies heavily on me. I need to rest. I lie down, wrap myself in the bedcovers, and fall into a deep sleep, an escape from everything.

Chapter 3

I wake, terrified. I just dreamed I was driving a long way for an important meeting with senior staff in an office block outside the capital. When I got there, I realized just before I got out of the car that I had forgotten to put my sandals on. I was in a tight spot and couldn't think what to do. Anyway, what I do at least know now, waking up in this room, is that this is real and not a dream itself like I thought it was. I try to go back to sleep, but hear a phone ring. I turn to the phone beside me, but realise the ringing is not coming from there. I remember my double in the room next door. The ringing comes from in there, and it's still going on. I go to the door, bend down and peep through the keyhole. I am not there, I mean he is not.

How long have I been asleep? I don't know. There's no way to tell the time, or even the date. All I know is that we are in January, maybe mid-January. I haven't been worried about the date in the last few days. I've been on holiday and determined not to worry about what time it is, or what I time I go to sleep or wake up. The ringing stops, and then starts again. I go back and peep through the keyhole. There's no-one in the room.

I have to find a way to get out. I look right and left, wondering how to do that and notice the book by the side of the bed. I remember my unease about opening it. Maybe I'm anxious about what I might find in it. I pick it up and open it. After the cover there's a page that has my name under the title in neat handwriting. On the next page, there is a single, centred paragraph headed 'Introduction'. The text says: "In a small room, in an unknown place, someone is peeping through a keyhole at someone peeping through a keyhole at someone else in the room next door. They are all spying on other people endlessly, and that's all they are doing." I don't understand what this strange introduction means. I turn over the page. The next one is blank. I look through the rest of what is a huge book, but am surprised to find all the pages blank. I close the book, and return it to its place, wondering whether I am really the author of a one-paragraph, weird or ridiculous book. What a joke!

I peep through the keyhole again. "I" haven't come back. I sit back down on the bed and think about my family. They won't notice I'm missing for at least a fortnight. I said, before I left, that I'd be away that long and that they should leave me to it. I told them: "I'm off somewhere to be in solitude, to purge myself of everything. I'm leaving my mobile off the whole time. I'll do without it." I recall now I didn't take my mobile with me when I went out for a walk last night. I try to recall anything else from last night, but my mind's a blank. Something has made me forget what happened afterwards. I remember that Mahra is the only person I told where I'd be, and I even told her the hotel room telephone number. I wonder if she'll notice I haven't been in touch. Will my not being in touch bother her? Will she contact the hotel to ask after me? Is she thinking about me now?

Chapter 4

I need to get out of here. I stand at the door yelling: "Can anyone hear me?" I listen hard, but no-one responds. What's going on? Is this where it ends, in a room next to one containing someone who looks exactly like me? Or is someone having a really bad joke at my expense? I go over to the door and bang on it violently. I pause a moment, then yell: "Please open the door! Don't make me break it down!"

Still silence. I feel crushed. What am I going to do?

I go to the fridge and take out a bottle of water and an apple. I eat the apple and throw the core in the bin. I drink some of the water. After eating the apple, I thought it had tasted a little off. I wonder if the food and drink might be poisoned. I considered making myself throw up, but then changed my mind. Why would anyone trying to do away with me choose that bizarre method? Why would they lock me up like this if they were? If I had any enemies I could recall, I might suspect them of it, but I couldn't think of anyone.

I put the bottle back in the fridge and go back to the bed, dwelling on my solitary confinement. It reminds me of something that happened to a neighbour friend of mine when I was a kid and he was a year younger than me. I went around to his house one day to play. For some reason or other that I forget now, he locked himself in a room and couldn't open the door. He was screaming and crying hysterically to be rescued, but I couldn't seem to help him. Then his brother came along and told him to push the key under the door so he could open it for him. When he opened it, we went in and we saw he'd wet himself out of panic, and I could tell how embarrassed he was that we'd noticed. His brother started laughing loudly, and I went straight back home. When we were grown up, the neighbour told me he'd dreamed of locking himself in that same room again for many years afterwards.

Now I hear the door in the next room opening. It must be him. My double. I jump up and make for the keyhole. I bend down and peer through it. He puts a number of books on the bedside table. When he takes his outer clothes off, I notice he has my underwear on. He takes these off in the same way I do. He is now completely naked. That body is my own! I mean it's my body, my arms, and my legs. How could someone else have an exact copy of my body? Is that how I look when I dress and undress? Those broad shoulders; those ugly-looking patches of dark skin; that bushy pubic hair. I seem a stranger to myself when he undressed before my very own eyes. I used to think my body had no defects. Maybe I used to avoid looking in the mirror. I never once thought of ugliness in my own body that I would be able to see by looking at it naked from a distance. I always used to tell myself that clothes hide many a deformity, a conclusion I drew from that time with the skirt. It was some girl sitting in some place I can't remember now. The short skirt showed off her saggy inner thigh. If her skirt had been just a little longer that flabbiness would have been hidden and her beauty preserved in my eyes.

I'm still following him through the keyhole. He's turned all the lights out except for one faint light shining from somewhere or other from the corner of the room. I can still make him out, though. He pulls back the bed cover, and, naked, he gets in. He turns the reading light standing on the little bedside table on. Now I can see him more clearly. He's picks up a small book that was on the edge of the bed. I try to make out its title from the spine, but I don't know it. It might be Kawabata's House of the Sleeping Beauties. If only the light were brighter, I would be certain, especially as it's one of my favourite novels.

Stillness prevails. I'll call him and maybe he'll hear me. I yell to him and watch him through the keyhole: "Can you hear me? Let me out of this room! I'm begging you! Why am I locked in like this? And where am I? Who brought me here?"

But he carries on reading, turning the pages like a deaf person. I stand in front of the door and hammer on it with my fists. I yell at the top of my voice: "Can't you hear me? I want to get out of here! You've locked me in here for no good reason. You've violated my liberty!" I bang even more violently on the door with my fists. Now I'm really frightened. I cry until I'm exhausted, then stop and pull myself together. I wipe the tears away with my palms, and look through the keyhole. He's still reading, with a strange kind of coldness. I feel pain in my back from bending and peering too often, and go back to lie on the bed. It must be late, late enough at least to have to read by a faint light. It can't be daytime, because you don't have time to read and take an afternoon nap. I wonder if he knows I'm here. Is he spying on me? I remember that famous TV programme, Big Brother, where a group of people are filmed living in one place. Is something like that happening to me? I survey the ceiling looking for hidden cameras, but don't see any.

I go back to thinking about that "me" in the next room. I haven't heard him speak yet. How could I, since he's alone? I might hear him if someone else gets in touch. That also makes me feel tremendously afraid. I feel like very alone, cut off from life, from humanity. It's like I've been cast out, and that my life is going to end in this place, pitifully, wretchedly. I can smell death in the room now. I can taste its bitterness in my mouth. My heart is beating violently like a bird struggling to get out of its cage. I curl up on the bed, close my eyes, and doze for a few seconds until I suddenly awake, again with fear. I'm afraid he'll come into the room while I'm asleep and kill me. I think it over a while and dismiss the idea. If he had wanted to kill me, he would have already done so by now. It seems he has some other plan for me that I don't yet know about. I say a few prayers then give in to sleep, as I usually do in the face of one crisis or other.

Chapter 5

I don't know how many hours I've slept. Maybe I just dozed a little. I get off the bed and bend down to spy through the keyhole. My double is sleeping on his back with the bedclothes off. That must be how I sleep. For the first time, I feel the need to go to the bathroom. I go in, relieve myself, and come back out. I don't feel sleepy. I decide to observe him until he wakes up. I kneel down and look through the keyhole. My pain in my back comes back again. If there were a chair in here it would help. I look around and spot the small table on the right side of the bed. I take the book and phone off it and place it under the keyhole. It does the job. I sit observing him. My double tosses and turns but doesn't wake up. I don't know if I do the same as him, especially as he is sleeping heavily, as I generally do. This kind of surveillance seems a little boring. I go over to the fridge and pour a carton of peach juice down my throat. I go back to watch again, but soon feel once more bored, so I decide to get undressed and go to bed like he's done. Our beds are identical, even down to the coverlets. How can the same man sleep in two different rooms at the same time? Were we born twins and our parents abandoned us? If so, which of us, if either, lives with our real family?

I recall José Saramago's novel, *The Double*. It tells of a man who sees someone that looks exactly like him playing a bit part in a film that he rents from a video shop, and was recommended to him by a friend. His double is a hotel receptionist. After a great deal of effort, he finds his double, but discovers that in real life he's a bad person, who only brings him troubles. What if the same scenario is happening to me? What if my double wants to do me harm?

I convince myself these thoughts are the typically stupid and pointless ones that come to me just before sleep. In the morning, as usual,

I'll laugh at them. But my thoughts still race away. I think about my sleeping double next door. Will you wake up and spy through the keyhole at me sleeping? Or will you open the door to observe how I sleep?

I recall that paragraph written in the book beside me, with my name on it. It was about spying. Is my life here to be solitary, in a room with a keyhole that lets me spy on someone who looks just like me in the next room, all being orchestrated by one or other of us? Am I part of all this surveillance? But the one I'm spying on acts normally and I don't notice him spying through a keyhole at me or anyone else. Does it make any sense for him to spy on me or anyone else like that?

I still suspect a camera is watching me from somewhere. It doesn't have to be in the ceiling. It could be an ultra-sensitive miniature camera in the wall or that painting, just like those spies use in books, newspapers, and films. I turn the light off, and am in complete darkness. I strain my eyes to look for any point of light that might lead me to a camera, but find nothing. I turn the light back on and check around the room, on the ceiling, in the corners, around the bed, in the bathroom and in the fridge, but find nothing suspicious. I take the painting off the wall and examine it closely back and front. I check over the telephone thoroughly, then pull the cable out of the wall socket, and put the phone in the bathroom as a precaution. It might be bugged.

I surrender myself to my fate. I tell myself they can film and do what they want. I'll see how this calamity that I've fallen into works out. I remember my sleeping double and hope I wake before him so that I can see how he wakes, or, put it another way, how "I" do. Mahra's face appears before me. I long for her so much now. I pull the bedclothes completely over me, and fall sleep.

Excerpted from *Ghurfa Wahida La Takfi* (One Room is Not Enough),
published by Difaf Publishing, Beirut and Algiers 2016.
Longlisted for the 2017 International Prize for Arabic Fiction

LAILA AL-ATRASH

Hymns of Temptation

EXCERPT FROM THE NOVEL

TRANSLATED BY NANCY ROBERTS

From the Papers of Father Mitri Haddad, April, 1940

How shall I begin my letters to you, and when will you read them? During my lifetime, or after I'm dead and gone? I haven't decided yet.

Am I writing so that you'll understand and pardon? Am I confessing because I seek forgiveness from the Lord? Or is it just that the country is at a critical crossroads and we need to record our testimony to what we know?

Whatever the case, I'm going to write as though I am talking to myself, since you're a piece of my soul.

I'm at a loss as to how to begin. I don't even know what to call you, or what sort of address could bridge the void between us. And the disclosure I need to make terrifies me.

Shall I address you as my beloved son? Of course. For surely you are beloved to me, more than you could ever imagine, and that is despite your belief that I don't love you, or your mother before you. You'll never know what joy filled my life the day you were born! A short-lived happiness, the Angel of Death stole away with it as your mother lay bleeding and delirious, her brow beaded with sweat. The childbed fever that took her begrudged me the joy I'd been blessed with through your birth. Her death shattered me, son, more com-

pletely than you could never imagine. It also burdened me with guilt. I suspect that if the Almighty had prolonged her life, your presence might have brought us closer together. But God willed otherwise.

Believe me, Rafiq, she didn't distract me from you and your mother. My love for her was a cross that I bore on my own Via Dolorosa, a preordained fate inscribed on my brow that was my bliss and my wretchedness alike.

Like death, love launches its arrows wherever it wills. Neither time nor place can avert it. Neither power nor prestige can stand in its way. It holds nothing sacred but its own bidding.

When I saw her before the altar, I became guilty of disobedience right then and there. I transgressed one of the ten commandments. I coveted my neighbour's wife in my heart. Deep down I felt a shudder that ill befit a servant of the Lord. It was a feeling that tormented my conscience and kept me from being fully devoted to your mother, as I wasn't completely hers anymore.

Forbidden passion is an unruly steed. No bridle can restrain it or halt its onrush. The more sharply you rein it in, the more stubborn its disobedience and the louder its neigh. After all, the shackles of reason are loosened by the lure of love.

Right then and there, my heart was caught in love's satanic grip, and all my amulets were rendered powerless. It is a wretched man whose mind's affairs are ruled by his heart.

My love for her now stood between me and God, and you had escaped my grasp.

Unbeknown to you, I squandered my days and nearly drove myself blind searching for a path that would bring you back to me. I would gladly have slaughtered the fatted calf in celebration of your return as the bereaved father in the famed parable did for the prodigal son. You've been gone a lifetime, it seems, and the distance between us is filled with salt marshes and paths too rugged to traverse. So now I don't know what to do, or how to get you back.

When you're in the centre of a circle, you can't determine its circumference. Only those who stand outside it can measure its extent and reveal what lies within it. You closed your circle to me, while I stood trapped in an endlessly revolving circle of my own. Fooled by your calm exterior, I couldn't see how lost you were, and I defended my rights over you by treating you all the more harshly, while your own harshness blocked your way back to me. Whenever you began to draw closer, you were drawn away again by your belief that I'd been unfaithful to your mother, and your sense of abandonment dug the furrows of alienation between us all the deeper.

A crown of thorns encircles my head, and a spear is lodged deep in my heart. You come home at dawn reeling, and brush off my angry questions with hateful nonchalance. If you do respond, you stumble over your words, and your speech is slurred. "Markus's Tavern is the only truth in this life," you drawl, "and everything else is a bunch of

In **Hymns of Temptation**, Rawia Abu Najma – a documentary producer who has not visited Jerusalem since the Six Day War of 1967 – obtains a special permit to return. Although she has come to sort out the affairs of an aged aunt, she secretly hopes to make a film about people's lives in the city. Through her aunt's memories and those of her friend, the wife of the custodian of the Holy Mosque, a forbidden and passionate love affair between her aunt and the priest Mitri Haddad comes to light. She also uncovers old disagreements between the Greek Orthodox Church, Muslims and Arab Christians in Jerusalem. The novel charts the social development of Jerusalem and the struggle of different peoples to control it, describing life from the period of the Ottomans and the British Mandate at the end of the 19th century to after the Israeli occupation. It is a novel of people living through times of sweeping moral, political and social change.

goddamned hypocrisy."

When you say things like that, you might as well throw me into a pit of despair. Where did you get the illusion that your world is devoid of love, or that drink will give you the solace you crave?

Love disappointed is as hotheaded and cruel as hatred. The dreams I had cherished concerning you were falling apart already, and then you'd launched a frontal attack on them. But how could I have gone so far as to strike you?

From defeated, fleeing Turkish soldiers anxious to rid themselves of anything that might betray their identity, your grandfather had bought a leather strap along with some pistols and rifles. Then he'd hung them on the wall as a reminder of that bleak period of our history. Gripped with fury, I took the strap down off the wall and lashed out with it at my disappointed hopes, the hopes I had pinned on you only to find you choosing a path entirely different from the one I had wanted you to.

Afterwards I was tormented by remorse, and wished I hadn't found that strap hanging next to the door.

With bitter rage and a thirst for revenge, I reached out for the strap, but just as I took hold of it, you shouted: "You've got no authority over me! As far as I'm concerned, you're not even my father!" As the cruel truth sunk into my heart, my grip loosened and the strap fell to the floor.

How could you have hated me so much that you were willing to drown yourself in a bottle of booze and disown me to my face?

A fit of rage and a shot of whisky will bare the soul, revealing the things hidden deepest in a person's heart.

I walked the short distance between the Mutran School and Bab al-Amud. My spirit, already weighed down, was crushed by the head priest's words, and I stumbled over the crumbled fragments of my soul. His looks accused me of having been too busy for you, and I felt so crazed I couldn't see, crowned with the shame of failure. I didn't know you had been gone longer than the regulations allowed, which suggested that I was negligent and didn't care whether you came back or not.

Why, Rafiq?

It's not easy for someone like me to cry and beg for mercy, son. In any case, the head priest gave me one last chance with you.

You can't imagine how harshly I was criticised, or what a dagger sank into my back the day I enrolled you in the Sisters of Zion, and then in the Mutran School. After I escorted you to school on your first day there, Dhimyanous reprimanded me, saying: "When our priests drag their children to schools run by other denominations, can't you see what shame this brings on us?They stand at their doors begging them to let them in!"

"I don't care about inter-religious feuds," I told him. "All I care about is what's good for my son. Our schools have gone downhill, so we have no choice but to take our children elsewhere. My son is just as good as boys of a different denomination, and I won't deprive him of a good education just because his father is a priest. Besides, I'm no more fanatic than the Muslim sheikhs and Jerusalem notables who've enrolled their children in schools run by other denominations."

The Truth has ways of its own that are beyond our reckoning, so they take us by surprise, and we feel scattered and confused.

You've often been harsh toward me, Rafiq, but I forgive you. I can understand why you didn't want to be around me. At the same time, I pray for God to soften your heart toward me and her. It isn't fair of you to hold her responsible for a crime she didn't commit. You seem to think that my love for her kept me from loving you and led me to betray your mother, and I excuse you for that. Your mother's death was the will of God, but what you had to go through after she died is more than any little boy should have to endure. Certain ignorant women hinted that there was some connection between your birth and your mother's passing and accused you of being bad luck. My God, it was terrible! I'm sorry to be exposing you to the sorts of things people have said, but I promised to write as though I were talking to myself.

I preached sermon after sermon forbidding the sort of cruel, superstitious things certain women were saying about you, but they kept up their malicious gossip all the same. So is that why you held me responsible for your mother's death? Did it give you a sense of relief to blame me for something I had no control over? In any case, you and I both ended up being miserable over a crime neither of us had committed. How could you have believed that she died of grief when life and death are in God's hands alone?

What I want you to know is that I honoured your mother till her dying breath just as a good husband should! God knows I never once fell into bodily sin. On the contrary, I resisted temptation and Satan's lure. Even though it was a struggle, I was faithful to your mother in body till God took her to Himself. As for the heart, no one but its Maker holds sway over it.

Believe me, son, never once while your mother was alive did I speak to anyone about my romantic attachment or what I went through in that connection. I endured my ordeal alone. So how did she learn of it? I have no idea, and I never dared ask her, may she rest in peace. She was extremely intelligent, good-hearted, and sensitive. My suspicion that she knew tortured me no end. Sometimes I could see a word of reproach suspended from her lips or glimmering in her eyes, and I'd be torn apart inside just as I knew she was. So we would avoid each other's glances. She never did utter that word of reproach, and I never asked her what she was thinking. Did she have a sixth sense that enabled her to pick up on her man's hidden feelings? Or did I say the other woman's name in my sleep one night? I don't know. However, I can be almost certain that she confided her suspicions to a friend who didn't keep her secret.

Whatever the case, to put your mind and heart at rest, I call upon God as my Witness that I never voiced my feelings even to the people I love until years after your mother's death, and after my decision to change my life and leave the priesthood.

I'm going to talk to you about this man to man.

What drove me to this other woman wasn't physical desire, and I didn't break the laws of the Church for the sake of urges I couldn't control. Rather, I came to feel she was a piece of me that had become separated for some reason, or that a part of me had been recreated and had been incarnated in her. I felt at home with her, like a helpless little boy who runs for protection to a mother who's as lost and confused as he is. Whenever I saw her I was born again. When I was with her, no shackles fettered my soul, and I could be a boy, a man, a teacher, a father.

There's nothing like feeling you're the whole world to a woman, that she looks at everything through your eyes alone like a deprived little girl who finds protection in your embrace. Despite the cruelty of the years that had passed, she still had the ability to possess my soul.

The first time I saw her, I realized then and there that a demon of sorts was drawing me into a terrible temptation. I could see him standing with me on a precipice overlooking a deep abyss, just as Satan stood with our Saviour on the mountain top and subjected him to the severest test a human being had ever endured by offering him the kingdoms of the world in exchange for denying his Lord.

I neither succeeded nor failed. The temptation to which love had exposed me brought me to a treacherous slope, but I neither fell nor maintained my foothold. Instead, love cast me into a circle that pulsated with endless questions.

Big questions are torture. May God protect you from questions that might plunge you into a sea of doubt, rob you of the blessing of tranquility, devour your spirit and its inner peace. Like an eagle consuming its prey, doubts have ravished my mind. Questions have sunk their talons into my spirit and ripped my faith to shreds. So, does God subject us to temptation to settle accounts with us? Weren't hearts made to love? Isn't God love? Haven't we been commanded to love even our enemies?

The most beautiful love of all is forbidden passion, against which the world and its laws release their most violent fury. We suppress it until we wither up inside, or until we become unrecognizable to ourselves or others!

Bound by passion, my soul longed to be free. But the more violently I struggled to break loose, the more tightly it held me. When I prostrated in devotion, all that appeared in my mind's eye was the face of the woman I longed for. Like a soul mate that refused to leave my side, she inhabited my dreams, my worship, nay, my every waking moment.

Believe me, Rafiq, there is no justification for the grudge you hold against her. She had no hand in what we've been through, nor did she have any knowledge of my feelings until I spoke to her about them. Now, since I swore to write truthfully, I admit that her swift response took me completely by surprise. As though she already knew how I felt and had been expecting me to approach her, she showed no hesitation at all. She wasn't known for being reckless, and nary an insulting word about her had been heard. Yet she threw herself headlong into the arms of love and embraced its consequences, the sweet and the bitter alike.

Did your mother's death signal the beginning of a new destiny? Now don't be angry, son! The length of your mother's life had been determined before you were even born, just as my torment was preordained before I ever saw the light: "O God, life and death are in Thy hands!"

I decided to leave the priesthood, but my path was strewn with obstacles. Whenever I rolled a boulder aside, another one would appear in its place.

"Our church can't endure another scandal!" Dhimyanous shouted when I approached him about my desire to leave the priesthood. "We've already seen one priest released from his vows on account of women and the lusts of the flesh. We can't have another priest do the same thing! The other denominations will never let us hear the end of it! As you may know, we're still reeling from the scandal that broke over Brother Ashil when we couldn't keep him under control. Another scandal would be too much for us."

Have you heard Ashil's story? He was a bright, handsome young Greek monk with the Brotherhood of the Holy Sepulchre who had risen to the highest rank of the priesthood. This came as no surprise, however, as his sister was married to an influential Jerusalemite, a poet and man of letters from a well-known family whose ancestors had been among the denomination's most generous benefactors. He was also Dhimyanous's closest friend and companion.

Brother Ashil fell head over heels for a Greek girl by the name of Sonya, the daughter of one of Jerusalem's most prominent jewel merchants. Hers was a rare beauty, and whenever she walked down a street, heads would turn. Ashil fell so completely under her spell that he forgot who he was and to whom he had devoted himself. When the Greeks fall in love, they do it in style. The monk's eyes betrayed the flame ablaze in his heart, and he was swept away by a passion that nothing could stop. Before long Jerusalem was in an uproar over this monk who had abandoned his worship and gone trailing after a young girl, up and down the city streets. He spent his days waiting on her doorstep and carpeting her path with his agonized longing wherever she set foot.

No passion is more violent than a love forbidden, and deprivation has a way of taking the heart over until it beats for nothing and no one but its beloved.

"God made Sonya just for me, and I'm going to obey my heart's command," Ashil declared to the enraged patriarch when he was summoned for a reprimand.

Then, without waiting for the patriarch's decision, Ashil cut his hair, removed his frock and turned his back on his religious duties to devote himself entirely to the one he loved. As for the Greek beauty, she preferred the young man who'd vowed himself to God over the hordes of others, Arab and Greek alike, who had coveted her favour.

It wasn't long, however, before envious glances had twisted the love story between the monk and the young beauty into a tale of lechery and depravity, and on spiteful tongues it became an ignominy that stigmatised the Orthodox Church.

So Ashil was expelled from the priesthood.

Seeing what had happened, I went before Dhimyanous and demanded to be released from my vows, too.

My demand was a just one, I argued. After all, I reasoned, since they had allowed a Greek monk who occupied the highest rank in the priesthood to be released from his vows, then they certainly wouldn't mind if a lowly Arab priest like me did the same.

Dhimyanous somberly heard me out. Then he asked me to give him some time, saying: "Let us pray for God to open up a way for you to leave, something that will enable the Church to save face and at the same time keep you from falling into sin."

The Fates like to toy with human beings, amusing themselves with people's uncertainty and their fear of what the future holds.

Who would ever have imagined that Ashil's and Sonya's tempestuous love affair would end up uprooting everything around them, and that the ardor of a Greek monk would decide the fate of an Arab priest?

That year the denomination suffered a series of setbacks, including a new scandal related to the first one which shook the foundations of the patriarchate, undermined the denomination's respected position, and blocked the way to my deliverance.

A lovely, unmarried Greek nurse, who happened to be Sonya's maternal aunt, had treated a Russian archimandrite at the "Moskkubia" Monastery in Ein Karem who was suffering from mild paralysis. She lived with him during the treatment, which lasted for some time, and tongues started wagging both in the village and beyond. In an attempt to redress his error, the archimandrite compounded it with a second error that turned into a resounding scandal. As the saying goes "He came to put medicine in her eye, and blinded her instead!". He gave the nurse a house that had been set aside as a church endowment so that she could leave the monastery, saying: "It's a reward for her selfless service to me and for standing by me in my illness."

Thereafter the young nurse proceeded to turn the house she'd received from the Church into a wine tavern, which became a gathering place for Jerusalem notables at whose boisterous, drunken nightly celebrations Ashil and Sonya were in regular attendance. So, was what this woman did her way of avenging herself on a town that had ruined her reputation? Or was it a way of securing quick wealth that she could take back to her country? God knows.

When Dhimyanous exiled Ashil and Sonya to Greece, the Russian archimandrite took revenge by doing even worse things to embarrass Dhimyanous and to exacerbate the enmity that had arisen between the Russians and the Greeks when the Muscovite churches split off from them. He rented the "red house", an endowment belonging to the Russian Society, to Fakhri Nashashibi, who brought his Jewish mistress to live there.

Dhimyanous said to me: "If we're going to preserve what's left of the priesthood's prestige, you'll need to leave the country until people have forgotten about Ashil and the Muscovite. Besides, going away would be a way of testing your feelings to see how genuine they are. It might also help you to get over them. By the time you return, God will have shown us what is in the Church's best interests. But at the present time, the Orthodox Church couldn't bear the scandal of having another priest leave to get married."

No true love would ever end by force of an edict, be it religious or secular. The Creator alone has power over hearts that throb with passion.

"Thy face, O Lord, do I seek. Hide not Thy face from me."

After leaving you in the care of your maternal grandmother, I set sail in quest of my salvation in the Monastery of the Garden of the Holy Virgin on Mount Athos in Greece. I remained in seclusion observing the sea, a hermit devoted to the worship of his Lord, singing hymns of miracles morning and evening.

Her image went before me and inhabited the caves in which I performed my devotions. She appeared before me in my prayers as a painting on the monastery walls. She nested in trees that stood guarding the sea, and blanketed the surface of the water. Try as I might, I couldn't set myself apart in purity.

"The Lord is my light and my salvation. Whom shall I fear? The

Lord is the stronghold of my life. Of whom shall I be afraid?"

Living among ascetics devoted to the worship of God only increased the heaviness in my breast. Their otherworldliness and self-denial made me feel all the more sinful. So in the end I came back to Jerusalem to be released from a vow I had made to myself only to find that I lacked the ability to fulfill it, and a vow to my mother that had become more of a burden than I could bear.

"Your Grace, my soul continues to impel me toward her, and I cannot withstand its force. For years I have resisted the urge to disobey. Not a moment passes when I am not assailed by temptation, and I can bear it no longer. If you fail to release me, Venerable Father, you will bear my guilt."

At length he replied: "After considering the matter thoroughly, praying to the Lord for wisdom and direction, and consulting with the monks of the Brotherhood of the Holy Sepulchre, God has led me to a decision that I hope will be for the good. You should know, of course, that I place the good of the Church over any other consideration. What I have concluded is that the reputation of our priesthood could not survive a third scandal, nor could our Church. At the same time, it is our duty to spare you the sin of adultery by not depriving you of her. As you are well aware, adultery is the gravest of all sins before God. It is forbidden by the Ten Commandments, and under ecclesiastical law, it is grounds for divorce. Because the laws of the Church forbid a widowed priest to remarry, and since our circumstances do not permit us to expel you from the priesthood, we are obliged to resort to the lesser of two evils. That is to say, we are of the view that despite the sacredness of the Church fathers who laid down the laws of the priesthood, they, like us, were mere human beings and, thus, subject to error. Violating an interpretation put forward by human beings, however elevated their station and profound their knowledge, remains less serious than violating the laws of God. And God is my witness that our purpose in committing a breach of this magnitude is solely to prevent a new scandal from inflicting further harm on our priesthood. Rest assured that my love for my Church is the only thing that could possibly motivate me to allow such a serious transgression. This is the second time I have committed disobedience for your sake. First I lied to the Ottomans to save your life, and now I'm going to allow a widowed priest to remarry to protect the priesthood and to prevent him from committing adultery."

I knelt before him and kissed his hand. Dhimyanous had decided my fate, and I had no choice but to bow to his verdict.

"My only condition," he continued, "is that you swear on the Bible never to divulge the matter of your marriage to anyone whatsoever, not even your son. You and your wife must not live together under one roof, and neither of you must weaken before the harshness of people's words and suspicions. Patient endurance of others' cruelty and suspicions will wipe away your guilt. And although this woman never conceived by her first husband, you must exercise the utmost caution. We will not tolerate a still greater scandal."

Our wedding ceremony was held in Dhimyanous' house, and it was witnessed by the housekeeper and her Greek husband.

I kept my vow of secrecy, and as we had been prepared to expect, we were eaten alive by wagging tongues. You lost your way because of people's whispers and gossip, and by the fact that the truth was being kept from you. I was often tempted to confess to you. In fact, I felt like shouting from the rooftop that we were husband and wife. But then I would remember the vow I had made. I thought of leaving Jerusalem with the two of you to get away from it all, but I couldn't think of a convincing excuse. I also held back because I thought you were happy with your school and your friends, and that staying where we were would be the best thing for you. So I put up with people's suspicious, hostile glances. In fact, I became addicted to them. When you get used to something, you come to accept it, and when other people get used to it, they stop talking about it after a while. I stayed with you thinking I was making you happy. Little did I know that your spirit had long since left the city behind.

Jerusalem has caused us to lose our way because she's so much like us. Like us, she has two faces. Her ancient streets lead to the gates of salvation. She seeks forgiveness in churches, in monasteries, in temples, in hospices, in mosques, in synagogues, in prayer rooms. At the same time, however, she opens the gates in her wall to pleasures that lead to perdition.

Was my spirit healed by being near the person I loved? For a time, yes. But then it wandered away with you on the paths of your turmoil.

Excerpted from *Taraneem al-Ghiwaya* (Hymns of Temptation),
published by Difaf Publications, Algiers, 2014.
Longlisted for the 2016 International Prize for Arabic Fiction

SINAN ANTOON

The Colloquy of the Birds

EXCERPTS FROM A NOVEL,
TRANSLATED BY JONATHAN WRIGHT

Photo by Samuel Shimon

I can still remember the first time I flew. "Come on. It's time!" my father said firmly before flying off. My mother pushed me gently toward the void with her beak and whispered: "Don't be frightened, my little one. You'll fly. We all fly. I'll be right behind you."

My three siblings were flying happily in the sky, oblivious to me. My heart was pounding, as if it were also worried its wings might let it down, as if, like me, it was torn between the fear inside me, which kept me in or close to the nest, and an overwhelming desire that compelled me to be like the grown-ups.

I moved forward warily to the edge of the branch, which dipped a little with my weight and the weight of my mother behind me. I didn't look down. I looked up, where my father was circling in a clear, cloudless sky. I spread my wings, then looked back toward my mother. She didn't say anything this time but her eyes gave me courage and she kissed my head with her beak. I remembered how she had often told me that we have strong wings and that my wings would one day carry me to distant lands. I looked ahead and plucked up all my courage and flapped my wings with vigor.

And I took off.

I couldn't believe myself. I flew with confidence, as if I had often flown before. The cold air swept past my white feathers. The whole sky was mine and the whole world was laid out below me. With a flip of a wing I could twist and turn, rise and fall. I kept flying till the sun bade us farewell. I was the last to come home that day.

I laugh now, and I'm embarrassed too, when I remember that moment and the fear that later left me. Here I am now, flying with the grown-ups for days on our journey to the warm lands.

* * *

A drop of sweat fell on the edge of the piece of paper and I stopped reading. His handwriting was neat and confident. The ink was black, maybe from a ballpoint pen. The words were perched like birds on lines that looked like small sky-blue threads running across small brown pages. I thought of this because he had written about the sky and flying. The passage reminded me of the storks' nest I used to see in Shorja on the dome of a building when I was young. I turned the page. The title of the passage that followed also began with the word "Colloquy".

The air-conditioning unit in the room was panting and sputtering, and the pores of my skin were oozing sweat from the heat. I wiped the drop of sweat off the page with my finger and caught another one that was rolling down my forehead and about to drop. I left the pages on the bed next to the buff-colored notebook, stood up, went to the air-conditioning unit and turned the dial anticlockwise as far as possible. I went to the bathroom and washed my face in cold water. I dried it with the towel and went back to stand in front of the air-conditioning unit for thirty seconds. I thought about the long tiring journey to Amman. I had to get packed and sleep a little, because we were scheduled to leave Baghdad at six a.m. I went back to the bed and read his letter a second time:

> Dear Mr Nameer,
> I hope you had a productive day in the arms of your tired Baghdad. Apologies for intruding and daring to disturb you. But I've thought long and hard about the happy coincidence that brought us together and about your sincere interest in my project and your kind offer to translate it (although I'm not in a hurry to have it translated or even published, as I mentioned, at least not for now). I have decided to take a risk and lay claim to more of your generosity and kindness. I sat down waiting for you at the hotel reception until half an hour before

Index/Catalogue tells the story of Nameer, who meets Wadood, an eccentric bookseller, in Al-Mutanabbi Street during a brief visit to Baghdad after the 2003 occupation. Wadood is working on a vast project, an index/catalogue detailing the minute-by-minute history of the war from the perspective of rocks, trees and animals as well as humans themselves. Taken with the bookseller and his project, Nameer tries to contact him to find out more, with the aim of writing a novel about him after his return to the US. Influenced by Wadood's ideas, Nameer begins to observe his mother country as it fragments, collecting newspaper clippings, images and everything relating to Iraq. Meanwhile, Wadood is on the edge of insanity and trying to gather the broken splinters, sounds and ghosts of his surroundings. Will he succeed in rescuing them from oblivion?

the start of the curfew so that I could deliver this part of the manuscript to you personally, but you didn't come back. That's why I'm writing this letter. I attach the first chapter (it's the history of the first minute, which has not finally ended, and I have views on completing texts that I might tell you about in the future). I hope you like it and I hope you'll give me your opinion with the candor of a critic and a writer, even if it is negative.

With this letter you'll find a simple gift, because books are all I have in this world. I'll try to obtain an email address so that we can communicate across the continents and the oceans. Thank you in advance and I apologize again if I was a little rude at the beginning of our meeting. I'm not usually much good at dealing with people and I prefer books, because they don't hurt you or betray you.

With affection,
Your brother,
Wadood Abdul Karim,
Baghdad,
July 29, 2003

He's not interested in being translated or published. So why is he sharing his manuscript with me so readily? Does he care that much what a stranger thinks? He's strange, this Wadood. I folded the letter up and put it in the notebook I had bought specially to record my impressions of this visit. It had large pages that were slightly brown. The edges were stitched and trimmed unevenly to look like an old book. It had a thick cover of buff leather and a thin red ribbon attached to the top of the spine as a place marker. The marker was still on the first page, where I had written just one word since arriving: Baghdad.

I envied Wadood his productivity. I don't know how to start. In the end all this concern, or rather obsession, with writing rituals and instruments leads only to blank pages and silence. This visit had of course been hectic and hurried and the pace of the work and the daily travel exhausted me physically and mentally, leaving me no time to write or even to think calmly. I hadn't yet started to deal with the whirl of scenes and people and ambivalent emotions. Even so I should have written something. One sentence at least. Every night I came back tired and sat on the bed. I picked up my pen but didn't manage to write anything. The first night was the only night I wrote anything – that one word Baghdad.

I went back to thinking about his manuscript and his gift, which wasn't simple at all. It's true that it wasn't the first edition, but only the second, but it was the first part of the collected poems of Mullah Abboud al-Karkhi, and it does date back to 1956 and I think it's rare. The book is in excellent condition. I browsed through the first few pages. There was a dedication to King Ghazi and a picture of the king on the next page, then a picture of Mullah Abboud al-Karkhi. The introduction was a collection of tributes and essays: there was a poem by Maruf al-Rusafi entitled "To the Poet of the Nation" (What a fine man you are, Abboud / With your rhymes you raise the banner of *zajal**), another poem by al-Zahawi, an essay by Raphael Butti on colloquial Arabic in poetry and prose, one by al-Rusafi on *zajal* poetry and popular forms of literature, another one by Mohammad Bahjat al-Athari on colloquial and classical Arabic, and then finally the poems themselves. As I expected, "The Crusher", his most famous poem, was the first in the collection. I fell asleep before I was halfway through and dreamed that al-Karkhi was our driver on the journey to Amman. All the way he recited his poems and explained their background and context, but Roy kept insisting that I translate them. I lost my temper with him and said: "Poetry can't be translated that way. We're not at a press conference!" And I kept repeating, "One hour and I'll break the crusher / And curse this damned way of life", and al-Karkhi roared with laughter and said: "How did you get involved with them?"

I woke up to loud banging on the door of my room and Roy's voice saying: "Come on, Nameer. We have to leave in half an hour. Don't you want breakfast?"

I had a shower in record time, dressed hurriedly and stuffed the rest of my clothes and other things into my bag. I hadn't bought anything other than the books from Mutanabbi Street and my bag was big enough for them and the box of cookies that my aunt had given me. I put Wadood's envelope, my notebook and the Karkhi poems in my backpack with my passport. I hate to be late for a departure or for any appointment but I had another reason for hurrying, a much

* Zajal is a form of traditional poetry recited or sung in a colloquial dialect.

more important reason. I wanted to savor one last time *gaymer*, the Iraqi-style clotted cream, and the hot bread that arrived fresh every morning from a bakery close to the small hotel in Karrada. When I went down to the ground floor Roy was going over the bill with the receptionist, who spoke enough English for them to understand each other, and I was bored of translating. "Do you need any help?" I asked him anyway. "No, everything's fine. You have some time because Laura's still packing and needs twenty minutes. The driver hasn't arrived yet either."

I put my bag next to Roy's big bag close to the front door and went to the hotel restaurant, a small room with four tables and a door that led to the kitchen. Abed the waiter saw me from inside the kitchen and we exchanged greetings. I sat down at a table on the right, turned my cup over, took a Lipton teabag from the plate in the middle of the table and put it in the cup. If it had been real tea, from a teapot and flavored with cardamom, the breakfast would have been perfect. In America I had moved away from drinking tea, especially after I moved out of my family's house and switched to coffee. Two minutes later Abed arrived carrying a tray with a small bowl of *gaymer*, another bowl with date syrup and a blue plastic basket holding two loaves of bread. He put the tray on the table in front of me, then went back to the kitchen to fetch the hot water for the tea. He hadn't spoken much, except for the first day we'd had breakfast, a week earlier. He asked me at the time about my travelling companions.

"Excuse me, sir, but the group you're with, what's their story?" he said.

"They're married and they've come to make a documentary," I replied.

"Really? A month ago there was a group of French people staying here who were making a film. Very well, and you would be the director?" he asked.

"No, I just came with them to translate for them and help them."

"Do you live abroad?"

"Yes."

"Where?"

"In America," I said.

"How long have you been away?"

"Since 1993."

I asked him about his work.

"I've been working in this hotel for four years," he replied. "Our house is in Camp Sarah but for the last few months since the fall of Baghdad I only go there once a week. I sleep here."

We didn't speak after that because he had been busy with his work and because over breakfast Roy, Laura and I had discussed the day's schedule and the places we were going to film.

Now as he poured hot water into my cup, he asked: "It looks like you're leaving today, sir?"

"Yes, that's right."

"Hope you have a safe trip. Which city do you live in, sir?"

"In Boston," I said. "But in a week's time I'm going to move to a state called New Hampshire," I added for precision.

"I've never heard of it, to be honest."

"It's on the border with Canada. Very cold," I said.

"The cold's easier to take than this heat. What do you do there?"

"I've got a job at a university," I replied.

"Congratulations. I hope it goes well." I expected him to ask what my discipline was, but a voice called him from the kitchen. "Excuse me, sir," he said politely.

I put two spoonfuls of sugar in the cup of tea and stirred it. I took a sip that almost burned my tongue and put the cup back in place. I took a loaf of bread, split it open along the side and spread cream inside, adding two spoonfuls of the date syrup. Abed didn't come back. I ate slowly to enjoy my last breakfast. I had tasted this Iraqi *gaymer* in America on a visit to San Diego, where many Iraqis live, but it tasted different there. This cream reminded me of Umm Jalil's, which she used to leave in a bowl on the stone bench by the door early in the morning. I remembered how a stray cat had had its nose in the cream one morning and lapped some up. Would Umm Jalil still be alive? I examined the sole picture hanging on the wall opposite. It was an attempt to draw a traditional Baghdadi backstreet. There were women in abayas carrying baskets. In the background there was the dome of a mosque, a minaret and a sunset scene. The colors were garish and there were unintentional mistakes in the perspective and the proportions of the objects. It was an attempt to produce a local authenticity but it fell into the trap of auto-Orientalism. I reproached myself silently for the way I was speaking and over-analyzing. There I was – thinking like an academic even before I officially started my new job. I had seen many of these paintings in the city, sold to journalists and newcomers. I remembered that the department head had asked me in an email to decide what course I planned to teach, apart from giving Arabic lessons, so that it would be added to the curriculum, and I had to decide quickly. The woman who had held the position before me had taught a class on Andalusian literature. The department head suggested I teach that too and then I could propose another course for the following year. I didn't have enough time to prepare a new course, and Andalusian literature would be an opportunity to reduce the number of questions on terrorism and jihad, which intruded on every class and lecture.

I began the rituals of preparing another piece of bread and cream but Roy's voice called from reception. "Hey, Nameer. Laura's ready and the driver's waiting," he said. I finished the sandwich, wrapped it in a paper napkin that was on the table, put it in one of the pockets of my backpack and drank the cup of tea, which wasn't quite so hot.

Mullah Abboud al-Karkhi wasn't in the driver's seat, just Aboul Aref, the Jordanian driver who had been with us throughout the visit and who worked on the Amman–Baghdad route and knew the Iraqi city well. Roy and Laura sat on the front seat next to the driver while I took the back seat, which allowed me to stretch out and go to sleep.

Baghdad was still yawning and sleepy. Most of the shops had their eyes shut. There were some people on the sidewalks but the streets were semi-deserted. A car drove past us from time to time. American tanks and armored vehicles were lurking at the junctions. I noticed the words "US Army Go Home" written in red paint on a wall. It was me who was going back to the country the US Army came from and I looked likely to stay there. I was going back to a country that was not yet "home", even after a full decade. On other walls I had read expressions of gratitude to the Americans that made me sad. I wanted to see the Tigris and say goodbye to it. I didn't know when I would come back, or if I would ever come back. How dull the Tigris had seemed on this visit. It no longer looked the way I remembered it. But did anything still look the way I remembered? Nothing had managed to escape turning dull. A pigeon fancier had woken up early to let out his flock and watch the pigeons circle in the city sky. Seeing the birds in flight suggested an answer to my question – an answer that gave wing to a simple joy. The pigeons were still as they were – beautiful and free . . . free at least for this fleeting moment.

The pigeons reminded me of the stork in Wadood's manuscript. I thought about him coming to the hotel and leaving the manuscript for me. It struck me as a rather strange and impulsive gesture. Or was I exaggerating and being too hard on him? Hadn't I asked him to write to me? Hadn't I offered to help? My sudden return to Baghdad with these Americans was also strange and impulsive. Had I come to rediscover something, or to make sure it was lost? Wasn't I ill at ease in this city and in a hurry to leave? Had I come back to examine the wounds I had left behind, or what? I wanted to read the rest of the manuscript, but not now because I was exhausted and sleepy. Later. It was a long way to Amman.

I woke up after about two hours to find desert stretching away on both sides of the road. I asked the driver where we were and he said: "We passed Ramadi an hour ago. The others are sleeping too." I looked at them. Laura's head was in Roy's arms and his head was resting on the small bag that he used as a pillow.

"Didn't they stop us along the way?" I asked.

"No," he said, "only at the first checkpoint at Abu Ghraib."

"How long to the border?" I asked.

"You've got al-Rutba in an hour and a half, and then about an hour after that we get to the border." He paused and then, looking at me in the big rearview mirror and half smiling, he added: "What? You're that impatient to get out of Iraq, Mr Nameer?"

He took every opportunity to make bad-tempered and malicious remarks. Twice I had argued with him angrily and I had raised my voice so loud that I upset Roy. On one occasion I had confronted him saying: "You love Saddam." He had been evasive, saying: "No, but I'm not with the Americans." I had replied, "What makes you think I'm with the Americans?" but then decided there was nothing to be gained by arguing with him.

"No, Aboul Aref," I said. "That's unfair. Haven't you ever had a passenger who asked where we are and when will we arrive?"

"Just joking," he laughed.

I was going to tell him that I missed being myself and on my own. I was tired of translating everything that was said. I had spent six whole days with them: Roy, Laura and Aboul Aref too. From early morning to sunset we had gone round and round doing interviews and filming. They were pleasant and working with them was easy, but six days were enough. The day before had been the only day when I was able to breathe and move around freely. Aboul Aref took them to Nahr Street and the copper workers' market to buy gifts, walk around the markets and then have some grilled fish to eat. I had gone to Mutanabbi Street to wander around and buy books. After that, I went to our old house and then to the house of my aunt, who had prepared a meal of stuffed vegetables for me and invited relatives for me to meet. She pressed me to invite "that American group that you're filming with" but I told her I preferred to come alone.

"They don't speak Arabic, Auntie," I said, "and if they come I'll have to keep translating for them and I won't be able to enjoy myself with you. Besides, they're busy tomorrow."

"As you wish, then. Good, do you remember our house? Can you find the way on your own?"

"Of course I can, what do you mean?" I said.

I used to go there as a child in summer and play with my cousins and spend the night there days at a time.

I walked a little, then took a taxi from al-Rusafi Square to our house in Amin al-Awwal, which later had its name changed to the Gulf district. I wanted to take a look at it and say hello to any of our neighbors who were still there. When we were about to approach the Amin Bridge I asked the driver not to cross to the other side of the canal because the street that leads to the house is directly on the right. The cars slowed down and we saw a traffic jam in front of the street that leads to our neighborhood. Some of the cars were turning and driving back toward us in the opposite direction. There were some Hummers and American troops waving the cars back. The driver wound down the window and shouted at one of the drivers who were coming back.

"What's going on?" he asked.

"The street's blocked," the other driver replied, "and they're not letting anyone in."

He looked at me with a sigh.

"I know another way," I said. "We can go back and get in near the court and through the backstreets."

"Are you sure?"

"Yes."

He turned the car around and we went back and drove into Court Street. We turned at the traffic circle and took one of the streets leading to our street, but then we saw a Hummer parked at the end of the street. There was a man standing outside his house with a child and I asked him what was going on.

"They've been sealing off the area for an hour," he said.

I thought of getting out of the taxi and walking.

"Are they letting pedestrians through?" I asked him.

He shook his head and said, "No. No pedestrians and no vehicles."

The driver was looking at me and expecting me to pay the fare, so I asked him: "Can you take me to Beirut Square?" And he agreed.

I felt a lump in my throat. I had wanted to have a look at the house and the street I played and ran around in. I had thought I would knock on the neighbors' doors and ask about my childhood friends. The taxi driver didn't speak throughout the journey.

I wiped my sweat away with a handkerchief I was carrying after he dropped me off in front of my aunt's house. I saw three cars parked on the pavement. I pressed the bell outside, then pushed the metal gate, which was a little rusty and had flaking white paint. The garden wasn't as lush as it had been. My aunt's husband, who had died three or four years earlier, had treated the garden as sacred ground. I noticed they had added some rooms to the second floor. There was a separate entrance with a staircase. My aunt came out through the front door and started make a trilling sound. Her face was just the same, except for the wrinkles. But most of her hair had disappeared beneath a black hijab that she hadn't worn before I left Baghdad. Wiam, her eldest son, came out behind her. I later learned that he and his wife and children were living on the second floor. She cried as she hugged and kissed me, and started to tell me off, of course.

"You should be ashamed that you've been here a week and you only come on the last day," she said. "We haven't seen you for ten years. Don't you love your auntie any longer, you rascal?" "The man's a doctor now and you still call him a rascal,"Wiam told her. I gave him a kiss and said: "I'm not a doctor yet. My dissertation isn't finished yet." He laughed and said: "All but a doctor."The others were waiting inside: my cousins, my other uncle and his wife and their children and their wives and children. I greeted them one by one and tried to remember the names of the children, and the people I hadn't met before. As for the adults I had known before, time seemed to have crushed them like a steamroller, as if they had had to live through the last ten years several times over, back and forth, and had endured massive doses of pain.

"Why don't you stay with us for a few days, my dear?" my aunt asked me as soon as I sat down.

"Unfortunately I have to go back to Amman tomorrow."

"You mean, you couldn't put off traveling for a few days?"

"No, Auntie, I have to go back. I have a stack of responsibilities. I have to move to a new state and get ready to teach."

When I had called her to tell her I was in Baghdad, she wanted me to leave the hotel and stay at her house. "Aren't you ashamed to come to Baghdad and stay in a hotel? Bring your American friends to stay at our place. We can make room for them. Bring them over," she said.

I told her that the filming schedule wouldn't allow it and they had to charge the batteries for their equipment every night and so we had to be in a place where there were no power cuts. "We have a generator, my dear," she said.

My uncle, a retired engineer, was the only one to ask about my dissertation and the academic work I was about to start. The others bombarded me with questions about America and life there and what would happen in Iraq in future, as if I knew or was in direct contact with President Bush. Like the people whose words I had translated on camera for the past six days, my relatives were divided over what had happened. There was no consensus, even on the right term to use: occupation or liberation. There was an acrimonious argument between the men while my aunt supervised the preparation of the table. One of my cousins turned to me to ask me what I thought. He didn't like what I said and asked: "So you came out, too, to demonstrate against the war?"

"Of course," I said.

He laughed and said sarcastically, "You are so spoiled, man. If you'd been living here with us all these years, even if the Angel of Death had come to liberate you, you would have welcomed him."

"America is the official agent of the Angel of Death," I said.

"No way! So why do you live there?" he asked in a loud voice.

"Enough," his father rebuked him, "you've gone too far!"

My aunt called from the guest parlor: "That's enough arguing. Come and eat."

I asked her about the tablets I'd seen her putting in the water jug and she told me it was to sterilize the water because otherwise it would cause diarrhea. She put plenty of stuffed vegetables on my plate, especially the stuffed onions because she knew how much I loved them. Then she said: "Is there food like this in America?"

"Where I live there aren't any Iraqi restaurants," I said.

"You've been living as a bachelor all these years, so why haven't you learned to cook?" she asked.

"Sometimes I cook, but not stuffed vegetables."

After lunch we went back to the sitting-room. I felt quite exhausted and could hardly keep my eyes open, but I pretended to follow the discussion against a background of teacups and the sound of drinking. My aunt saved me by suggesting I take a siesta on the sofa in the guest parlor under the opening of the air-cooler: "Where you used to sleep in summer when you came here, remember?"

I smiled. "Of course I remember. Yes, please."

I took off my shoes and socks, put my head on the pillow she brought me and slept for an hour and a half. Then I woke up, washed my face and went back to the sitting-room. We chatted at length and drank tea again with the cookies my aunt had made specially for me. She gave me a full box to take with me.

Before I said goodbye to them, my aunt pulled me by the arm and asked to speak to me alone. When she was alone with me she told me off for cutting off my father and not speaking to him for years. I asked her if she knew the reason and what he had done to my mother.

"It doesn't matter," she said. "Whatever happened, he's still your father. Be magnanimous and don't break his heart. For my sake, Nameer. When you get back, speak to him."

I didn't want to disappoint her so I promised to think about it. That was a white lie, like my promise that I would soon come back for a longer visit without working or other commitments. She made sure she sprinkled water after me so I would come back. My cousin Medhat drove me to the hotel and gave me his phone number and email address before we said goodbye. The outer gate was locked but the guard recognized me and opened it for me. I greeted the receptionist, who was watching television in the room next to reception.

"Hey, man," he shouted, "there's a package for you."

He got up from his chair, came to the reception desk, bent down looking for something and then handed me a brown envelope. "Your friend Wadood," he said. "He waited here an hour and a half, and then he went and asked me to pass this on to you."

I was surprised. I thanked him, took the envelope and went up to my room.

* * *

Preamble (draft)

How can I write down what happened?

(This 'how' kept me up at night for many years.) And when I write it down how can it avoid the trap of distorting the truth and domination by the official history? I know there's something paradoxical and weird about it. Is it reasonable to start by worrying about the fate of what I write before my pen even spills ink onto paper? There's a wonderful African proverb in Chinua Achebe's novel *Things Fall Apart* that goes "until the lions have their own historians, the history of the hunt will always glorify the hunter". The idea isn't new, of course, but the metaphor is excellent, because it's always the victors who write history, and when someone comes along who wants to revise it, question it or change it, it's too late. But what about the history of the victim? That's what interests me. The first time I read that proverb I sympathized with the lion of course, but I thought hard about it and reconsidered, to discover, or rather remember, that I should take the side of the lion's victim. I imagined, even felt, that I was identifying with the gazelle (or any other prey) in this equation because it represents me and I represent it. I even feel I am it. I've been marginalized and taken out of the picture at least twice. I'm the prey's prey. But the numbers don't serve the purpose. The statistics may count us but in the best of circumstances they diminish our lives and our deaths. They dehumanize us. Assuming there's someone to count in the first place, because the historians of the hunt count the number of dead hunters! The numbers turn us into numbers. Dead signs and symbols in comparative studies designed to improve the hunt and make it more efficient. Our details disappear – our features, our color, our voices, our memories, our skin, our eyes and so on. Once we've been skinned, our skins might be tanned and hung on the wall in the hunters' homes. Or pictures of the hunters, standing next to our dead bodies to celebrate a new record, might be hung on museum walls.

But where should I begin, and how? Can I get inside time through a hole or through the window of one moment in time? I believe so. As soon as I get inside time, I can take the moment and analyze it as if it's a tear or a drop of blood under the microscope and discover the bonds and reactions that it produces. But how can I describe the moment when it isn't a moment, but in fact more like a tree? So I have to get down to the roots and listen to the earth's conversation with the tree and what it sucks from the earth. Then there's the trunk and everyone who has ever leaned on it or carved their name on it. And the branches and their memory and everything the wind has picked up and dispersed far and wide. And all the birds that have landed on it on their way to distant places. And the ones that have nested in it and so on. It's a maze. And which particular moment are we talking about? Is the moment the same moment everywhere? Or is each moment associated with its own place in the universe? If this last possibility is the case, then there is more than one time. There are times that might intersect but never coincide. But in this project I'm interested in one time in one place. Firstly I'll write down the history of the first minute of the war, which wasn't the first I've seen. Most of the people who take on history record centuries, decades and years. I'm interested in minutes, especially the first minute.

The minute will be a three-dimensional space. It will be a place where I snipe at things and souls as they move. The juncture where they meet before disappearing forever, without saying goodbye. Humans only say goodbye to those they know and those they love, whereas things say goodbye to each other and to humans too. But we rarely hear their voices, their whispers, because we don't try. We rarely notice things smiling. Yes, things have faces too, but we don't see them. Those who do see them, after making an effort and training themselves to do so, and those who talk to them go mad by your standards.

I'm the one who sees everything, and I see what they don't see. There's always a moment in the life of every being and every thing in which the whole truth about it comes to light. A moment when the past intersects with the future. And someone who can see and hear can discern the truth about that being. You no doubt sometimes see a photograph of a famous person, or even an ordinary person. And you realize that this picture/moment preserves the whole existence and history of that person. I'm not sure, but many of these condensed moments come just before death. I know I contradict myself sometimes. Is there any way round that?

Time is a black hole. A hole into which things fall and disappear. Even the beginning of this whole universe, according to one theory, was an explosion. And the universe is just fragments and debris, and here we are, living the consequences and effects of it. And I'm going to pluck this minute out of the black hole. But why? There are people who write in order to change the present or the future, whereas I dream of changing the past. This is my rationale and the rationale of my catalogue/index.

* * *

I liked his preamble, the idea of a history of the prey and a catalogue/index of the first minute. These were wild ideas that were not afraid of taking risks. He could elaborate further of course and set his mind to arranging the sequence of ideas. I jotted down some notes in my notebook. I kept reading as we waited at the Iraqi border post at Turaibil and again as we waited at Karameh on the Jordanian side. I had the idea of writing about Wadood and his project. It could be intertextual with his catalogue/index, including excerpts from it. Why not? But I had to find out more about his background and his life. I scolded myself for getting carried away with enthusiasm for an idea that was wonderful but totally impractical (when are wonderful things practicable?). I had to finish my doctoral dissertation to secure my job, and I had to turn it into an academic work, and after that I might be free for novels. That would be logical, but it's not my logic.

* * *

Aboul Aref drove me to the airport because my flight was due to take off in three hours. Roy and Laura planned to stay in Amman and visit Petra and Wadi Rum. "We need a holiday after all that pressure. It was so intense," said Laura, who often used the word intense, sometimes to describe things that deserved the word, but often for things that didn't. We embraced and I thanked them for the opportunity they had given me and reminded them that my offer to help them translate the film when it was finished still stood.

I don't know what came over me when I agreed to go to Baghdad after all those years. I would have done better to go alone at least, to ensure I had freedom of movement and could choose what I wanted to see, instead of being hostage to the team and its schedule, to which I was committed. But what was the point of all these recriminations now? There wouldn't be another trip. I had gone without expectations and thought I had immunized myself against any additional disappointments. I had read plenty about what happens to emigrants who go back after a long absence and, consciously or not, look for what is left. I had read about selective memory and nostalgia and its snares. But the texts didn't help much.

The Colloquy of the Caliph

Haroun al-Rashid's features were distinctive and anyone who saw him could not easily forget his face. His eyes were black. When he wasn't staring into space, his looks were piercing, and when he was angry they were glaring. And he was often angry. His eyebrows were gray, the same color as his mustache and beard, and they were bushy and much longer than necessary. He didn't have much hair left on his head, except around the temples. He had a brown complexion, wore a gray dishdasha over a pair of trousers and walked barefoot most of the time.

No one knew where the caliph lived. From his appearance, he didn't look as if he even had a home or that he owned many things other than what he was wearing. The street was his home, his palace in fact, as he used to shout emphatically at the top of his voice. He would scold the passers-by for daring to walk on his sidewalks without obtaining his permission or paying taxes. "This is Rashid Street, my street, the caliph's street, you motherfuckers, not your mothers' street," he would say. This shocked many people and they kept their distance out of fear. But those who knew the street grew used to him and knew that he wouldn't attack anyone physically, but would only shout and argue. The shopkeepers humored him and paid him a pittance in tax – some dinars or a cigarette for temporary relief from him and his shouting. He would go up and down the street shouting at the cars too. Sometimes he ventured further afield, went to the Martyrs' Bridge, where he stood in the middle, looked at the Tigris and shouted at the fish. Or he would look at the sky and shout, "Your god is full of shit." This latter expression upset many people and they would ask for God's forgiveness and some of them would rebuke him. But he would reply to them with another such expression in a loud voice.

There were several stories about the history of the caliph and it isn't possible to verify any of them. One version was that he was a rich merchant who had lost all his money after several loss-making deals and unwise decisions that had forced him to sell all his possessions in one year. After that he had gone mad. The other version said he had been driving his car at breakneck speed on the Mosul road and had collided with a truck. The truck's load had killed his wife and three children and he was the only survivor. The third version said quite simply that depression and madness had run in the man's family for generations. He had been placed in the Rashad Hospital for many years and it wasn't known how he had ended up in Rashid Street. But his real name probably was Haroun.

Haroun was inspecting the street corners, looking for one of his subjects or his ministers who, whenever they saw him, pretended that he wasn't the caliph. He wanted to rebuke them. He couldn't understand why his kingdom was uninhabited this morning.

Readers will be interested to learn that a short excerpt from this novel, then entitled "The Book of Collateral Damage", was published in *Banipal 34 – the World of Arab Fiction* (Spring 2009) when it was a novel-in-progress, not yet finished. The final version, entitled *Fihris* (Index/Catalogue) was published by Manshurat al-Jamal in 2016 and longlisted for the 2017 International Prize for Arabic Fiction. Its full English translation will be published by Yale University Press under the original title *The Book of Collateral Damage*.

VIKTORIA ZARYTOVSKAYA

Arabic Literature in Russia

The Beginnings

Translations of Arabic literature, philosophy, and other branches of knowledge, apart from the obvious interest enjoyed by the Qur'an, remained for a long time limited and out of reach for most Russian readers. Russian translators showed less interest in Arabic than they did in European languages; less even than some of the major languages of Asia. But recently, Arabic literature has begun to gain a foothold – albeit slight – in Russia's book market and libraries, and a general theory of Arabic-Russian translation has begun to take shape.

The first Russian translation of the Qur'an was produced in 1716 at the behest of Peter the Great, and was carried out by Peter Postnikov, a professor of philosophy at the

University of Padua and a native Russian. Though this was the first Russian version of the Qur'an chronologically speaking, it was based on the French translation by André du Ryer, not the Arabic original. It was beset by a number of errors and inaccuracies, beginning with the title, which was rendered as *The Turkish Law*. Moreover, it reproduced the mistakes of the French version, which the Russian translator did not bother to review, and suffered numerous omissions.

The next translation, produced in 1790, was essentially a revision of the first, reworked from the French version by the Russian playwright Mikhail Veryovkin (1732-95)). It is well known that Russia's great poet Alexander Pushkin (1799-1837) made use of this translation, which inspired him to write his collection of Romantic poems, *Imitating the Koran* (also known as *Koranic Inspirations*). In 1792, a third Russian translation was produced, this time based on the English version of 1734 by George Sale. This was the work of Alexey Kolmakov, who attended faithfully to the technical and semantic aspects of translation.

However, beginning in 1864, the translation of the Qur'an by K. Nikolayev became the most popular, going through a sixth printing. This version was based on the French translation by the Polish-French Orientalist Albert Kazimirski de Biberstein (1808-1887).

In 1871, the first direct Arabic-to-Russian translation of the Qur'an was produced by General Dmitry Boguslavskiy (1826–1893), a graduate of the Department of Oriental Studies at Saint Petersburg University. (Curiously, the name "Boguslavskiy" means literally "he who praises God"). Boguslavskiy dedicated his life to diplomatic service in Turkey. There are scattered references to various translations he made from Arabic, Turkish, and Tajik, yet unfortunately these remain lost without a trace. Even his translation of the Qur'an remained lost until its rediscovery in 1995. Until then, the version produced in 1878 by Grigoriy Sablukov, an orientalist and Islamic scholar from Kazan, was incorrectly assumed to be the first direct Arabic-to-Russian translation of the Qur'an. Sablukov's version had long been commended by linguists for its historical importance and the brilliance of its expression.

Subsequent translations of the Qur'an would be produced during the Soviet era, which brought changes both to Russia and Russian orientalism. The prominent Russian orientalist and academic Ignaty Krachkovsky (1883-1951) passed away before he was able to com-

A Thousand and One Nights

plete his translation. Yet the draft of his work, however incomplete, is valued for its precise and literal rendering of Arabic synonyms and structures. In addition, through his efforts at establishing a new Soviet school of Arabism, Krachkovsky helped produce a qualitative and quantitative leap in Arabic-Russian translations, especially literary works. This school established new methodological and theoretical traditions for studying Arabic literary and cultural heritage. Krachkovsky's writings on the then contemporary Arabic literature and culture of the late nineteenth and early twentieth centuries set the standards for scientific research in the field throughout the Soviet era. Scholars in Europe were also able to benefit from these advances. The well-known Russian orientalist Olga Frolova (1931-2015), a student of Krachkovsky's, celebrated her teacher's accomplishments in an eponymously titled book published in 2007.

Krachkovsky played a leading role in the Oriental department at the World Literature publishing house between 1919 and 1925. He described the work there as unlike anything he would experience before or since. The experience showed how fundamentally orientalist methodologies had changed since 1917, the year of the Bolshevik revolution that toppled the Russian monarchy.

Krachkovsky was involved personally and influentially in every project related to Arabic literature, whether as an editor or writer of introductions. Among the works he introduced are the following noteworthy titles: *The Testaments of Luqman the Wise*, *The Book of Contemplation* by Usama ibn Munqidh, *Hayy ibn Yaqdhan* (Ibn Tufayl's philosophical novel), *A Thousand and One Nights*, Ibn al-Muqaffa's *Kalila and Dimna*, *Ring of the Dove* by Ibn Hazm, and *Return of the Spirit* by Tawfiq al-Hakim. He also translated the odes of Al-Shanfara, which he collected under the title *Songs of the Desert*, in addition to the poems of Amin al-Rihani and the novel *The Days* by Taha Hussein. To appreciate the extent of his contributions to Russian Arabism, it is sufficient to quote Krachkovsky himself: "What is important for the discipline is that its foundations have been set, its rules and principles have been established, and its general contours sketched out."

Book by Naguib Mahfouz

A Turning Point

It is possible to speak of a first renaissance of Russian Arabism between 1929 and 1939, when the field was infused with independent initiative and creative energy. The translation of the *Thousand and One Nights* by Mikhail Salye (1899-1961) marked a turning point in translations directly from the Arabic, as the previous editions in circulation were adaptations from a French intermediary. This period also witnessed the production of a number of career specialists in Arabism and Arabic literary translation, including such luminary figures as the following: Anna Dolinina; Valeria Kirpichenko; Boris Chikov; Olga Vlasova; the famous journalist Leonid Medvedko; Dmitriy Mikulsky, president of the Center for Applied Orientalist Studies; and diplomat Vladimir Volosatov. We can also mention scholars and academics such as Vladimir Shagal, Igor Ermakov, and others. Russian Arabism managed to achieve its status thanks to the support of the Soviet state, which was interested in developing its relations with the Arab world.

The Arabic works that occupied Russian translators and Arabists can be divided into three groups. The first group pertained to the golden age of Arabic poetry and prose, and included the *Diwan* of al-

Book by Ghada al-Samman

Mutanabbi (916-965), the *Maqamat of al-Hariri* (1054-1122) and Badi' al-Zaman al-Hamadhani (969-1007), and a collection of assorted folk-tales.

The second group was comprised of prose works dealing with social and political struggles in the Arab region. These included works of so-called "resistance literature," as well as works by authors who had an ideological connection to the Soviet Union. Among the many authors worth mentioning here are Mahmud Taymur, Ghassan Kanafani, Abd al-Rahman al-Sharqawi, Ibrahim al-Koni, Tahar Wattar, and Ali Uqla Irsan.

The third group was comprised of authors whose works had earned international acclaim, including those who had been awarded literary prizes. They included Algerian writers Rashid Boudjedra, Assia Djebar, Mohammed Dib, Mouloud Mammeri, and Kateb Yacine; Egyptian writers Tawfiq al-Hakim, Taha Hussein, Youssef Idris, Naguib Mahfouz, Gamal al-Ghitani, Yusuf al-Sibai, Mustafa Mahmoud, and Mohamed Makhzangi; Iraqi writers Ghaib Tu'ma Farman, Dhu al-Nun Ayyub, Abd al-Rahman Majid al-Rabi'i, and Burhan al-Khatib; Lebanese writers Amin al-Rihani and Mikha'il Nu'ayma; Palestinian writers Ghassan Kanafani, Mahmoud Darwish, Muin Bseiso, Samih al-Qasim, Emile Habibi, Sahar Khalifeh, and Yahya Yakhlif; Syrian writers Adonis, Sa'dallah Wannous, Hanna Mina, Zakaria Tamer, and Nizar Qabbani; Jordanian writers Isa al-Na'uri and Fakhri Qawar; Moroccan writers Mohammed Zefzaf, Driss Chraibi, Mubarak Rabi, Mohammed Berrada, Mohamed Chukri, Idriss al-Khouri, Mustafa al-Misnawi, Abd al-Karim Ghallab, and

Tahar Ben Jelloun; Libyan writers Ibrahim al-Koni and Kamil Hasan al-Maqhur; Sudanese novelist Tayeb Salih, as well as selections from modern Sudanese poetry; Yemeni authors Muhammad 'Abd al-Wali, Abdallah al-Barduni, and Abd al-Aziz al-Maqaleh; Kuwaiti authors Laila al-Othman, Hamad al-Mazini, and Khalifa al-Waqyan; Saudi authors Abd al-Rahman Munif , Hasan Abdallah al-Qurashi and Abd al-Aziz Khuja; and Bahraini author Mohammad Abd al-Malik.

Book by Taha Hussein

* * *

In the 1990s, the collapse of the Soviet Union had a detrimental impact on Russian cultural organizations, including those involved in literary translation. The change was particularly severe in fields dedicated to the translation of non-European works. At this abrupt turning point for Russia, and under difficult economic circumstances, Arabic translation projects receded, and interest in Arabic literature reached its lowest point since its first bloom during the Soviet era. The situation was such that Arab authors were effectively cut off from their Russian audience, as their works disappeared from bookstores and library shelves. This cultural break with the Arab world created a vicious circle that would persist even after the return of stability to Russia. For just as the country was recovering from the pains of a difficult transitional period, the situation in the Middle East had become precarious, with new crises looming on the horizon. Meanwhile, due to its separation from the Arab East, the Russian street had become prac-

Book by Abdelrahman Munif

tically isolated from the events affecting its old friends.

At the same time, attempts to translate the Qur'an continued apace, as scholars strove to produce a more authoritative Russian version. Two translations appeared around the same time, both opting for a literary or poetic method of semantic interpretation. The first was Valeria Porohova's translation from the English, published in 1991. The second, based directly on the Arabic, was produced by the eminent Arabist and Orientalist scholar Teodor Shumovsky in 1995. Another translation of the Qur'an was published in the same year by Magomed Nury Usmanov, a linguist and member of the Royal Jordanian Academy of Sciences.

With the turn of the millennium and the renewal of Russian-Arab relations – albeit in different forms and pursuant to different interests than in the past – cultural exchange between the two sides also witnessed a rebirth. A new phase of translation, publication, and reception of the Arab author had begun. At the forefront of the Arabic translation movement have been the Institute of Oriental Studies of the Russian Academy of Sciences, and the publishing houses Oriental Literature and Nauka. One of the most significant works to appear in 2009 was that of Rifa'a al-Tahtawi (1801-1873) – *Takhlis al-Ibriz fi Talkhis Pariz* (*An Imam in Paris*), translated by the Arabist Valeria Kirpichenko.

The laws of the market forced Russian policymakers to change their behaviour. The principle of competition freed translation and publishing from the grip of the state and its onerous censorship regime, opening the door to new private and commercial publishing establishments. Translation was now subject to the law of supply and demand and other market forces. Under these circumstances, there appeared two new publishing houses that gave pride of place to translations of literature and other works from Arabic. The first, the Centre for Humanitarian Cooperation, concerns itself with the translation of modern literary works, as well as producing new translations of works that had been previously published. The second, Biblos Consulting, publishes translations of Arabic literature in addition to other works such as dictionaries, memoirs, and assorted nonfiction. The variety of translations put out by these two publishers indicates a focus on works that have gained fame in the West. As far as classical works are concerned, the Maqamat have been republished, as well as some poetic anthologies. Several works based on historical persons or events have also seen new editions, such as Jurji Zaydan's historical novel *Al-Amin and al-Ma'mun*. Yet classical Arabic literature has, on the whole, not received the same level of attention it enjoyed during the Soviet era. Most new translations and publications – and here we are still speaking of the two aforementioned publishing houses – are of modern novels, especially those of Naguib Mahfouz. The Centre for Humanitarian Cooperation has published three: *Wedding Song* in 2008, *The Journey of Ibn Fattuma* in 2009, and *Children of Our Alley*, which was re-translated in 2011. All are the work of the author of this essay, that is myself.

Book by Ghassan Kanafani

Other novels of interest to publishers are those that have gained

Book by Zakaria Tamer

notoriety within the Arab World and beyond, such as Youssef Ziedan's *Azazeel*. Translated in 2013 by Pavel Gulkin and Muhammad Nasr al-Din al-Jibali, it is the only recipient of the "Arabic Booker" to have made it into Russian. Two novels by Alaa al-Aswany have also been translated, due to the international acclaim they have received: *TheYacoubian Building*, translated in 2008, and *Chicago*, translated in 2012. Both are also my work.

A few authors of the new millennium have also been translated, besides those already mentioned: the Yemeni author Zayd Muti' Dammaj, Mauritanian author Musa Wild Ibnu, and Saudi author Hani Nakshabandi. Selections from modern Saudi literature have also been translated by Olga Vlasova. As for translations of the Qur'an, Elmir Kuliev's 2002 edition was highly acclaimed by experts. The most recent translation of the Qur'an was published in 2003 by the Arabist Betsy Shidfar.

The history of Arabic translation in Russia, from when it went past its long and difficult foundational period, through the emergence of academic Arabism with its endeavours in translation, especially the interest in the Qur'an, and more recently the downturn that has beset the field: all this deserves further contemplation and review. Indeed Pavel Gusterin, a scholar at the Institute of Oriental Studies of the Russian Academy of Sciences, provides a faithful account of the current state of Russian Arabism in his recent report, "Urgent Measures for Russian Arabism," and answers the questions that may spring to one's mind.

The Translation Situation today

We must first recognize that Arabic literature in translation was and remains only a modest presence in the Russian reader's library. Moreover, by way of comparison, it may be noted that Russia lags far behind European languages – English, French, and German – in its translation of Arabic books. From the perspective of any Russian Arabist familiar with the field, there exists a tremendous gap between the production of literature in the modern Arab World and its translation into Russian. Besides the sheer paucity of translations, there is the issue of keeping track of the latest developments in Arabic literature. Any shortcoming in this respect risks impairing the vitality of the translation movement, which depends on a comprehensive and continuous process of monitoring. One example of this is Alaa al-Aswany's novel, *The Yacoubian Building*. Its English translation appeared just two years after its initial publication in 2002, and was followed shortly by translations into a total of 34 languages. Its translation into Russian, however, did not occur until 2008, with a mere five thousand copies. This is of course not to discount the great socio-cultural differences that separate Russians and Arabs on the one hand, and those that exist between Arabs and Europeans on the other. The size of the Arab diaspora in Russia and the extent of their cultural activities can hardly be compared with the strength and vitality of Arab communities in Europe. Yet the market for books in Russia remains lively, and the Russian reader's appetite for foreign literature is quite strong. Such factors may help compensate for the dearth of Arab cultural activity and allow translation to fill the gap and achieve success both culturally and commercially.

Book by Ghaeb Tu'ma Farman

Another pressing issue, in our opinion, concerns the selection and promotion of translated works by Russian publishers. One finds that Arabic literature falls victim to the frenzied search for quick profits in the book market, and the desire to attract readers through shocking titles. Now and then, novels are promoted that present only a narrow subsection of Arab life, focusing on horror, murder, and mayhem. For example, the novel entitled *Burned Alive* by Souad, translated in 2009, deals with honor crimes in a nightmarish atmosphere, and similarly the novel *Disfigured* (2007), written by an author known only as Hadi. To be precise, we should admit that the authors of these works are not always Arabs, but their topics typically revolve around the Islamic world. Due to the paucity of actual and diverse works translated from Arabic, such novels are responsible for producing a distorted image of Arabic literature in the minds of Russian readers.

Book by Rashid Boujedra

All things considered, the average Russian reader's knowledge of Arabic literature remains quite modest, and is mostly limited to classical folk tales such as the *Thousand and One Nights*. It can be said without exaggeration that the latter is to be found in nearly every Russian home. Those with an interest in the Arab East (al-Mashriq or the Levant) possess a wider knowledge that includes pre-Islamic poetry – especially that of Imru' al-Qays – as well as later poets such as al-Mutanabbi and al-Ma'arri. When it comes to Arabists and those interested in modern Arabic literature, we generally find them discussing Naguib Mahfouz, the 1988 Nobel Laureate. As a result of these limits and gaps in knowledge, a general set of oriental stereotypes has cemented itself among Russian readers of translated Arabic literature.

Another issue that concerns the translation of Arabic literature in Russia is discussed by Mona Khalil, Director of the Centre for Humanitarian Cooperation. In an interview with the Russian magazine

Vostok (22 March 2015), Khalil explains:

"The first hurdle we faced in the publishing field was locating translators, at a time when Russian translations of Arabic literature were dying out. Certainly, there are many Russian Arabists involved in translation, only not in the field of literature. Arabic literature has not been translated into Russian for 30 or 40 years. There simply has not been demand, and so the number of specialists dwindled. As we know, literary translation is its own field, and specialists in it are quite rare. The other problem was with seasoned translators, who were eminent experts in the Soviet era, but whose style of Russian was dated and difficult to read today."

It seems clear that the neglect suffered by Arabic translation in Russia is due to multiple and complicated factors. When we speak of translation as having a socio-cultural essence, whose vitality depends on its connection to contemporary life, it is easy to understand how the weakness of Russian-Arab ties for several centuries has led to the incomplete absorption of literary texts. Literary innovation involves special semantic and technical issues whose expression differs fundamentally between Arabic and Russian, and these cannot be reconciled without genuine translation and the open exchange of knowledge between the two cultures. For example, whereas Russian style does not allow the repetition of the same word in two consecutive sentences, and disfavors chains of synonyms and adjectives, these features are perfectly acceptable in Arabic. There is also the obvious geographic division between Russia and the Arab world, and their distinctive cultural and linguistic traditions that make communication between the two sides difficult. Again, greater openness will allow for greater harmony.

Besides problems of a purely linguistic nature, there is the issue of text selection. Books chosen for translation are either uninteresting to the Russian reader, or impose undue burdens of language and style. That is to say, the translator throws the reader directly into the quandaries and complexities of the language without providing for a smooth and natural rendering of the text. This problem can be traced back to the old school of Russian Arabism, whose dominant approach was to the preserve all the linguistic and expressive peculiarities of the Arabic text. Their approach to their texts was based on sentimentality and aesthetic appreciation, formed from their long intimacy with Arabic language and literature. As a result, the translations they produced were an expression of their powerful feelings on Arab culture and the magic of the Arabic language. However, when considering these translations from the reader's perspective, one will find them full of constructions and clichés that make sense only to Arabic language specialists. The content and broader aesthetic quality of the text is thus lost on the average reader. Preserving the peculiarities of Arabic in translation is interesting as a linguistic experiment, and may attract those enchanted with the strange and exotic Orient, but it does not make for a serious and strategic translation venture.

Despite the existence of scientific methodologies for translating Arabic into Russian as well as the availability of university programs for studying Arabic language, the gap between what exists and what ought to be remains large. We are thus faced with two critical questions, at the very least: 1) Does this translation deficit not amount to a waste of all the experience accumulated over the years?; and 2) How will this impact the future of translation?

No doubt, the variety of literary creativity in the contemporary Arab World has great potential for translation in Russia. The rich cultural heritage that Arabic narrative draws on, the many developments it has undergone, its relationship with global literary movements, and the various social and political issues it addresses: all these elements are worthy of the attention of the Russian reader. This is especially the case for the current generation in this age of globalization. In addition, the last two decades of research in the humanities and its counterparts on the Arab world continue to acquire greater relevance on the global level, and this can be properly maintained only through translation. The tremendous amount of information about the Arab world that gets rapidly pumped out through television and social media onto the Russian consumer needs to be met with a robust critical awareness. This can only be developed through the translation of Arabic books, and especially works of Arabic literature. Finally, recent events indicate that Russia is keen to assert its presence in the Middle East, and this, presumably, should lead to more support for the translation of Arabic language and literature.

TRANSLATED FROM THE ARABIC
BY BENJAMIN KOERBER

Mohammed Hasan Alwan wins 2017 International Prize for Arabic Fiction

Valentina Viene reports from Abu Dhabi

The 2017 International Prize for Arabic Fiction was awarded to Saudi writer Mohammed Hasan Alwan for his novel *A Small Death* (*Mawt Saghir*). The novel re-invents the famous figure of the Sufi saint Ibn Arabi as a young man embarking on an inner and outer journey from medieval Spain all the way to Azerbaijan. Published by Dar al-Saqi in 2016, the novel was selected as the best work of fiction published in the last 12 months. Alwan had already been on the IPAF shortlist in 2015 with his novel *The Beaver* (*Al-Qundus*).

The winner receives USD 50,000 US plus USD 10,000 as one of the six shortlisted authors.

The other five authors were Libyan Najwa Binshatwan, with her important novel *The Slave Pens* about the untold history of black slavery in Benghazi during the Ottoman period; Kuwaiti Ismail Fahd Ismail, with *Al-Sabiliat*, a novel investigating the dramatic consequences

l to r, the six shortlisted authors: Mohammed Hasan Alwan, Najwa Binshatwan, Elias Khoury, Ismail Fahd Ismail, Mohammed Abdel Nabi and Saad Mohammed Raheem at the award ceremony

of the Iraqi blockade of the rivers flowing from Iraq towards Kuwait; Elias Khoury with his autobiographical novel *Children of the Ghetto – My Name is Adam*; Egyptian writer Mohammed Abdel Nabi with his novel *In the Spider's Room*, where he recounts the personal tragedy of Hani, a fictitious character unjustly arrested in a notorious incident in Cairo in 2001 and then released; and Iraqi writer Saad Mohammed Raheem with his investigation of Mahmoud al-Marzouq's life in *The Bookseller's Murder*, a novel that offers, amongst other things, an insight into the US occupation of Iraq.

The IPAF award ceremony took place on the evening of 25th April in Abu Dhabi and was also an occasion to celebrate the 10th award of this very prestigious award. Fleur Montanaro, the prize Administrator, highlighted the important achievements of the IPAF over its 10 years of awards as well as the growing numbers of entries, which reached the highest point this year with 186 novels being submitted.

Chair of judges Sahar Khalifeh holds up the winning novel

The chair of the judging panel, Palestinian author Sahar Khalifeh, spoke at the ceremony about the entries, expressing her delight in the huge creative effort of Arab writers today. She confessed to having discovered a plethora of young and less young writers who are willing to express themselves in often uneasy circumstances. She also expressed her frustration at bad novels not worth the paper they're written on – to paraphrase her – and called for publishers to be more selective and professional in the editorial process as their output shaped the Arab cultural scene.

After the screening of short videos about each shortlisted author, the announcement of the winner was made. In an atmosphere of great suspense and anticipation, Sahar Khalifeh slowly revealed the winning book, which had been concealed under a dark cloth. Alwan was then invited onto the stage for a brief speech in which he thanked the IPAF and all the institutions supporting the Prize.

At the ceremony the establishment of a forthcoming Nadwa in Oman was also announced: the workshop, joining two others already taking place annually in Jordan and Abu Dhabi, aims at supporting and encouraging emerging writers develop their creative skills and grants them some visibility, as some of the work produced will be published on the IPAF website.

At the press conference following the ceremony, Sahar Khalifeh revealed the difficulty of selecting one masterpiece from the shortlist, but asserted that Alwan's *A Small Death* excelled on account of the variety of aspects developed in it – that is, human, spiritual, historical and social aspects, and more importantly, on account of the language used. Alwan, prompted by a crowd of curious journalists, explained how he came up with the idea of fictionalizing the figure of Ibn Arabi and how parallels could be drawn between his times and the present one; he mentioned the five-year-long research he carried out on Ibn Arabi and the challenge posed by not being able to visit some of the places the Sufi saint travelled through. Only 10% of the book is based on facts, he said, but the more he looked into Ibn Arabi's life, the more fascinated he became about the human aspect of a personality who is, till now, loved by many and considered a heretic by others, a man who travelled more than Ibn Battuta and Ibn Jubayr and who stated, "Love is my religion". Alwan admitted he had initially planned to write a much shorter book and, although four chapters were removed in the editing, the final draft still reached almost 600 pages.

MOHAMMED HASAN ALWAN:
"In this book the choice of language was very important"

Banipal's reporter in Abu Dhabi Valentina Viene attended the ceremony award and conducted the following interview with the author of *A Small Death* Mohammed Hasan Alwan

How does it feel to have won such an important prize?

I am very excited. It is an honour and an opportunity to reach a wider spectrum of readers. Hopefully they will inspire me: I get inspired by my readers more than probably I inspire them. It is a push forward, much needed.

As the book hasn't been read in English yet, some people might have wrong expectations of what your novel is about. Could you tell us what A Small Death is and is not about?

A Small Death is a fictionalized life story of Ibn Arabi, the famous and very controversial figure in the Islamic history. Despite his fame and influence, we know little about his life as a human compared to what we know about his ideas, teachings, and theories. I tried to imagine what we don't know about him and write it in my book. The result is a very interesting story about a man who never stopped traveling for about five decades. What did he see? Encounter? Feel? And what kept him travelling for this long? These are the main pillars of the story.

Your novel is full of sarcasm and irony. Who is this irony directed to?

Sarcasm is not something I started to write with. In my first three novels, there was no sense of sarcasm at all. My fourth novel, *The Beaver*, is where I started to think that the character needs to be sarcastic. Here is a man who comes from a dysfunctional family, going through a mid-life crisis and he travels, meets a beaver and he starts getting interested in beavers because he hadn't seen one before. He discovers lots of commonalities between his family and the beaver, its social behaviour. Beavers destroy the forests to build bigger homes, and we humans do that, too. Beavers are very insecure. That's the same with humans. I started to throw all these parallels between the beaver and the family, even the way he looks at his sisters. I kind of discovered this voice in my writing and I liked it and kept using it. I got positive feedback about the readers about this new voice of me. However, it's also all about the context, what this particular novel needs, how it should be written. In *A Small Death*, sarcasm is present in parts of the novel where it's needed, the relationship between Ibn Arabi and his lifetime student, for example. Only when he got old he started to be himself, he wasn't the obedient student any more. He started to disobey the master. All of this has been written in a way that is supposed to be sarcastic. I tried to find the voice needed. Each story has its context and needs to be told in a certain way.

By using sarcasm, are you trying to criticise some behaviours, traditions, religions, ways of finding your own identity, rebelling against the older lot?

Sarcasm is not necessarily a means of critique. It could be, but it's not in my writing. Sarcasm is more the general atmosphere of a novel, a way to convey ideas.

What is "a small death"?

According to Ibn Arabi, Love is a small death.

The idea that love is the key to peace and harmony is much at the heart of Ibn Arabi's thinking. Does your novel embrace the concept?

Of course, from the title to the last page. Love, in a universal way, was a main driving force in Ibn Arabi's life and I cannot ignore that when I write his life story.

As you were looking into Ibn Arabi's life, did you find something of yourself in this searching soul?

You cannot be involved that deeply with a thinker like Ibn Arabi without getting influenced somehow. I cannot trace these influences precisely in my thinking, yet I can confidently say that writing this book has changed something inside me.

Are there similarities between our era now and his then?

More than I have imagined. Sometimes I feel that the only difference is merely technological. It is true that human societies evolve constantly yet this evolution is either very slow, cyclical, or embraces similar instinctual themes that never change.

You mention that you cut four chapters from the final novel, what have we missed out on?

Some detailed stories that I thought were redundant and boring. I believe they don't add value to the text so I don't think the readers are missing much.

Is there a specific audience you would really like this novel to reach?

No. I wish it is read by as wide an audience as possible.

Did you try to experiment with the language, the story being set in the Middle Ages?

The choice of language was very important, and a huge consideration as I was writing the novel. Everything we know about the people who lived at that time has arrived to us in written form, so people would write differently from the way they talk. I had to figure out how they talked, the daily chat, the gossip, the tones, the rules and norms, not in one city but in tens of cities, because he travelled from Spain to Azerbaijan, through so many places. That was very challenging, but it was necessary. It was very important to give the reader this sense that we are travelling with Ibn Arabi.

We are not just watching. We are seeing what he is seeing, we are hearing what he hears, even the smells – everything. So I carefully chose language that is more likely to be close to the true language they spoke, as much as I imagined it to be.

Did you use dialects? How was this done?

The novel is written in the first person. He has his own dialect, the way I imagined it, and he uses it throughout the novel. It goes deeper as he becomes more spiritual, he doesn't talk in the same way as he used to when he was young, but there are also other characters in the novel, coming from different countries, with different social statuses and backgrounds, so they have to have different voices. This is what I tried to convey to the readers, it's an effort on which the readers could agree or not agree with me. But for me, it was a very important consideration to assign the right voice to each character.

The Beaver *was short-listed at the IPAF in 2013, but you won with* Mawt Saghir *(A Small Death). Why do you think this one won, but not* The Beaver?

The Beaver was short-listed with five different novels, and selected by five different judges. We can't say that certain elements were missing in *The Beaver*. I believe that being shortlisted is more important than winning. Whatever comes from winning is fantastic, but the process of selecting the short list from all the books [submitted for the prize] is what gives value to those six novels. Out of 160-something books, these are the best six. Then, selecting one of these books becomes very subjective, because objectivity has played its role already in the first, earlier round of selection. There is an objective process of selecting the books and that's very important. As a judge, you can argue it out, you can defend this, but you can't really defend objectively the choice of one book out of six. That has to be subjective. These six books are six good books. Then it's all about your taste, your background, your emotions and all of that. Even the judges say that.

How did you come to publish with Saqi?

My first novel, *The Ceiling of Sufficiency*, was published in 2002. When I finished it, I was still a university student in Saudi Arabia, I

Mohammed Hasan Alwan at the Abu Dhabi International Book Fair 2017.
Photo by Samuel Shimon

was 22 years old. I sent the transcript to Saqi Books to ask to have it published, but they said no, it's not good enough to be published with Saqi Books. So I found another publisher. It was successful. With my second book [*Sophia*] I went back to Saqi and asked them "Can you publish this?" and they said "Yes, we can publish this one". So it got published. I published my second and third book with them, and then I asked them to re-publish my first one. I didn't want to continue working with my first publisher. They accepted my request and with Saqi I reached twelve editions of this first book. I always say to them: "Do you remember? You rejected that book". I have nothing against them, but I think it is a good story to tell those at the beginning of their writing career. You might get rejected and then accepted again later, so don't give up!

Has A Small Death *been translated into other languages yet?*

A week before the IPAF ceremony I received a request by an Italian translator. I am very excited about this. I would like to be read in Italian, in Italy.

You wrote A Small Death *in Canada. Would you have been able to write this novel in Saudi Arabia?*

I wrote three novels in Saudi Arabia and I'd say that they were more controversial than *A Small Death*. My novels are never super-controversial. I am not constantly probing and poking taboos, no. This is what my type of novel is, this is what I am focused on, so it's not that I am trying to avoid controversy. I haven't had a problem being Saudi. When I was younger, I found it harder to endure the criticism. That really affected me in my first book, the social criticism. The academics were praising my writing, they were happy with the novel. The positive feedback of the academics and the media is actually what gave me the strength to continue. On the other hand, some people were saying: "Oh, this is not right . . . the novel is revealing so much about religion and sex." I come from a conservative family, so I was shaken at the beginning. I asked myself if I was doing something wrong, if I should continue . . .

Could the novel be made into a film?

I don't see any reason why it couldn't be. There are tons of actions that take place in many places across the region from Spain to Azerbaijan. A filmmaker with sufficient resources could adapt the novel into an interesting movie or TV series.

Why do you write? What's the force that makes you want to write?

I write because I need to write. The reason for me is selfish. Of course, I want to write so my readers can appreciate it, and find value in it, but I always ask myself, if I didn't get published would I still keep writing? Yes, I would. My first book, I didn't think I would ever publish it. I didn't think at the time that it would ever be good enough to be published. I was under this impression, for the entire two years I spent writing those 400 pages, that I was writing so I could keep it, so I could go back to it at some point. I was writing to channel all these emotions I had. So when I finished and one of my friends said, "This is a nice book. When are you going to publish it?", I didn't really believe him.

And are you working on anything new at the moment?

Yes, but I can't tell you anything about it. I am just doing the research at the moment. It's going to be a historical novel, more recent than Ibn Arabi times, 18th – 19th century. I am trying to condense two or three hundred years into a novel that tells the story of five generations of a family. That's the intention.

What is your impression of the IPAF so far? What could be done better?

I really enjoyed my participation in Nadwa [the writers' workshop], both as a participant in 2009 and as a mentor in 2016. If there is something I wish IPAF did more frequently it would be the Nadwa.

Good luck with everything

Thanks

Becki Maddock reviews

The President's Gardens
by Muhsin al-Ramli

Translated by Luke Leafgren

Maclehose Press, April 2017
ISBN: 9780857056788, 352 pages. Pbk £12.99.
Kindle: £8.99.

Abdullah despised hatred

"In a land without bananas, the village awoke to nine banana crates, each containing the severed head of one of its sons . . . Each head had a story. Every one of these nine heads had a family and dreams and the horror of being slaughtered, just like the hundreds of thousands slain in a country stained with blood since its founding." So begins this tale of three friends, which also tells the story of Iraq, from before the Iran–Iraq War to the aftermath of the US invasion. Al-Ramli explores themes of friendship, family, loyalty, morality, humanity, secrets and destiny through a nonlinear narrative, which weaves together the stories of several individuals to tell an epic, multi-generational tale of a village and of a nation.

Abdullah, Tariq and Ibrahim are three friends, all born in the same Iraqi village in 1959. Known as the 'Sons of the Earth Crack', "they would almost never be seen apart from each other until destiny separated them in the days of the Iraq-Iran War."

Tariq, nicknamed "the Befuddled", is a cleric, who enjoys good living. He makes the necessary accommodations with the regime authorities and prospers in the village.

Ibrahim, "the Fated", is one of the heads in the crates. His catchphrase is "Everything is fate and decree", and he names his daughter Qisma, meaning fate. The relationship between Qisma and her father exemplifies the clash of the generations. Qisma rebels against

Muhsin al-Ramli

her father and against his acceptance of his fate. With the arrogance and optimism of youth Qisma changes her name to Nisma and strives to shape her own destiny, pinning her hopes on a young officer. But Ibrahim's fatalism has a limit and his apparent compliance with regime's wishes hides a secret and a bravery even he did not know he possessed.

Abdullah Kafka, who acquired his nickname through his tendency to philosophical pronouncements, is a device employed by the author to reflect on Iraq's situation. For example, he writes that "if Abdullah Kafka had spoken about this incident, he would have said:

'It was on the third day of the month of Ramadan, 2006. According to ancient history, that was when a strange amorphous blob with a giant body and a small head, called America, came from across the oceans and occupied a country named Iraq.' "Abdullah, the "prince of pessimists", is called up to fight against Iran and is captured. Following his return after years in captivity he is content to sit all day in the same seat in the corner of the village café.

The shocking discovery of the severed heads on page one grabs the reader's attention. Al-Ramli then goes back in time to introduce us to the three friends, and the other villagers and to describe the events that have led to this tragic, gruesome delivery. The dramatic opening of the first chapter is then reprised in chapter 27 and the consequences are revealed.

It takes some time for the novel's action to reach the gardens of the title, where Ibrahim secures work as a gardener at one of the President's many luxurious palaces. The luxury of the palace and gardens contrasts sharply with the lives of ordinary Iraqis, and with the horrors Ibrahim encounters there. The President's murder of a musician epitomises the senseless destruction of beauty and culture that Iraq has witnessed in recent years. Although the novel's Iraqi context naturally leads the reader to imagine that the ruthless, apparently crazy president is Saddam Hussein, Al-Ramli intentionally leaves the leader unnamed, thereby allowing him to represent the brutality of any dictatorship.

The President's Gardens was longlisted for the International Prize for Arabic Fiction in 2013. It is the third of Al-Ramli's novels to be translated into English.

Al-Ramli's last novel, *Dates on my Fingers*, focuses on the experience of Iraqi exiles, whereas *The President's Gardens* is set in Iraq and exposes the reader to the horrors of Iraq's recent history through the experiences of the villagers. However, readers who enjoyed *Dates on my Fingers* will likely also enjoy *The President's Gardens*. Both novels tell the story of Iraq in a poetic, philosophical style, and feature autobiographical elements, as do the majority of Al-Ramli's writings.

Muhsin al-Ramli is a novelist, poet, translator and academic who writes in both Arabic and Spanish. He was born in Sudayra in northern Iraq in 1967 and went into exile in 1993 after the government's persecution of his family, including the execution of his brother in

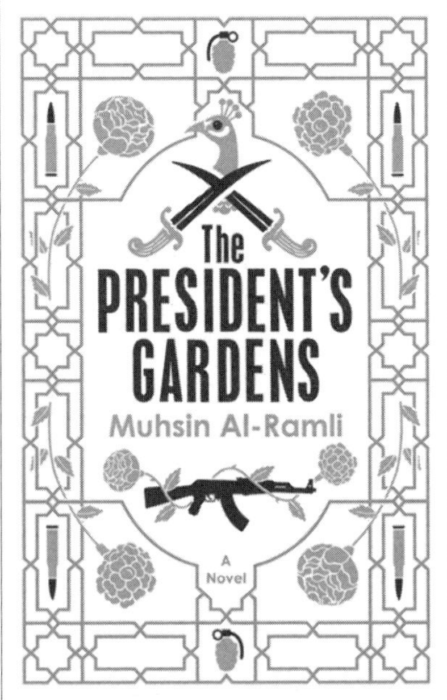

1990. He currently lives in Madrid. *The President's Gardens* is dedicated to Al-Ramli's own murdered relatives.

Al-Ramli hopes to introduce his readers to his native Iraq and his people, to personalise the familiar news stories, to make the victims individual human beings, not mere numbers. His novels describe Iraq's history as lived by its people, through its people. He uses his characters to comment on events. Examples include Ibrahim discussing the invasion of Kuwait with his friend Ahmad:

"Ahmad said: 'It's a depravity for them to kill people as they retreat and surrender!'

"Ibrahim said: 'It was depravity to invade our brothers and our neighbours.'

"Ahmad said: 'You know we aren't the ones who did that, and that anyone who refused was sentenced to death.' "

And this comment on the effect of sanctions: "The international sanctions hurt the common people most even as they consolidated the government's power."

Al-Ramli's touching and heart-breaking work exposes the senselessness of war and lays bare the torturing and murdering of Saddam Hussein's regime. The tone is not overtly angry, as one might expect and therein lies its power. It is a story of the Iraqi people that touches the heart and gives a human face to the news reports. Perhaps Al-Ramli shares his character's perspective . . . "Abdullah did not hate. He despised hatred and found no meaning in it. Hatred was just another burden on the soul. He wanted peace, nothing more . . ."

Susannah Tarbush reviews

Two volumes of memoir by Ibtisam Barakat

Tasting the Sky: A Palestinian Childhood

Square Fish, New York, 2016
ISBN 9781250097187 (pbk);
ISBN 9781429998475 (ebook) 208pp, US$9.99

Balcony on the Moon: Coming of Age in Palestine

Farrar Straus Giroux, New York, 2016
Hbk: ISBN 9780374302511, 240pp, U$17.99.
ebook: ISBN 9780374302535, 240pp,
ISBN: 978-1250144294, Square Fish, USA, pbk, Jan 2018

Growing up with war, exile, poverty and occupation

Palestinian author and poet Ibtisam Barakat's memoir *Tasting the Sky: A Palestinian Memoir* was widely acclaimed when it was published in 2007 by Farrar Straus Giroux, a division of Macmillan Publishers. The book was aimed at children and young adults, but had an appeal across the age spectrum. It received more than 20 awards and accolades, and has editions also in French, Spanish, Dutch and Farsi. Now Farrar Straus Giroux has published Barakat's sequel, *Balcony on the Moon: Coming of Age in Palestine*. At the same time the Macmillan children's imprint Square Fish has produced a paperback edition of *Tasting the Sky*.

Barakat was born in Beit Hanina, East Jerusalem, in 1964 and grew up in Ramallah in the West Bank. Her two beautifully crafted memoirs are written in a pared-down lyrical style. They trace the devel-

opment from infancy to adulthood of a highly intelligent imaginative girl with a passion for writing.

Ibtisam grew up in the challenging circumstances of war, exile, poverty and occupation. Against this tumultuous background she gives an intimate portrayal of a family and a society. Ibtisam's relationship with her mother is particularly finely drawn. When Ibtisam is three years old her mother kickstarts her love of writing when she draws with chalk the first letter of the Arabic alphabet. She tells her daughter "His name is Alef" and asks her to draw him.

"I thought Alef lived in chalk sticks," Ibtisam recalls. "Because I wanted to be friends with Alef, I took a piece of chalk with me wherever I went."

Alef is a recurring motif in Tasting the Sky. In the concluding section Ibtisam writes: "Dear everyone: Written on my heart, all that I lost – my shoes, a donkey friend, a city, the skin of my feet, a goat, my home, my childhood – shattered at the hands of history. But my eternal friend Alef helps me find the splinters of my life . . . and piece them back together." The book ends with Ibtisam's poem "A Song for Alef".

Tasting the Sky opens in 1981 with 17-year-old Ibtisam returning by bus to Ramallah from Birzeit, where she has been visiting her secret post office box in Birzeit. She has pen friends in various countries: "Having this box is like having a country, the size of a tiny square, all to myself."

The bus is held up by Israeli soldiers at a checkpoint, and driven to the Military Rule Center. Ibtisam witnesses the verbal and physical brutality meted out to the detained passengers by the soldiers.

She realises that under occupation it is Israeli soldiers, rather than her father, who control the family. "We are not free to be a family the way he wants, with him a lion in our lives. He is a lion in the zoo. Any of us can be taken away any day."

The incident leads Ibtisam to write for her pen friends the childhood memories that form the bulk of the book. The memories begin in Ramallah on 5 June 1967. The six-day war has begun and the family, terrified by Israeli aerial bombing, flees to Jordan. Three-and-a-half-year old Ibtisam gets temporarily lost because she cannot lace her shoes in time. The family spends several months in exile in Jordan, and is then permitted to return to the West Bank.

Ibtisam's mother cannot bear the stress of Israeli soldiers training on target practice near their house. Such is her desperation that she goes with her children to live in the Dar El-Tifl orphanage in Jerusalem and pretends that her husband was killed in the war. After the family moves home Israeli soldiers start making sexual advances to Ibtisam's mother and the book ends with the father moving the family to another area.

Balcony on the Moon, which was shortlisted for the 2016 Palestine Book Awards, tells of Ibtisam's teenage years. A main focus of this volume is the efforts of Ibtisam's mother to complete her own education with the help of her daughter. She had had to leave school early, and married at 15, because her family could not afford the fees. She asks Ibtisam to teach her everything she learns in class so that she will be able to enter classes at al-Urduneyyah secondary school, sit the Tawjihi (secondary school) exams and get a diploma. Ibtisam decides to help. "I am committed to teaching her as much as I am committed to my own studies." But Ibtisam's father is furious when his wife starts classes at the co-educational al-Urduneyyah, not wanting her to sit with men. His insistence she quit the school brings the marriage to breaking point.

During her teenage years Ibtisam becomes increasingly politically aware. She copies out the Universal Declaration of Human Rights, thrilled to find that "All these thirty rights belong to me, too!" Strong-willed and independent, at the age of twelve and a half she

Ibtisam Barakat

decides to uphold her right to work and to get a job in a paper factory, in the face of opposition from her father. She leaves in disgust after defending the rights of an old man who is being abused by a supervisor.

Ibtisam grows ever more conscious of her Palestinian identity, and witnesses demonstrations and the illegal unfurling of the Palestinian flag. She challenges a teacher on why she does not teach the history and geography of Palestine. The teacher tearfully explains: "If we teach about Palestine, we will be punished."

Ibtisam's love of writing leads her to prepare her own newspaper. She writes to the then editor of the Kuwait-based *Al-Arabi* monthly cultural magazine, Ahmad Baha' al-Din, offering her services as a correspondent. Moved by her letter, he gives her generous financial help and encourages her writing.

Balcony on the Moon ends with Ibtisam being ranked in the top ten per cent of the Tawjihi results. This grants her a scholarship for the first semester at Birzeit University, to study science.

Thirty-six years on, Barakat lives in Columbia, Missouri. According to her website her work "centers on healing social injustices, especially in the lives of young people." In addition to her writing, Barakat is a translator and educator. She translated two short stories by the prizewinning Palestinian author Isra'a Kalash for *Banipal 45: Writers from Palestine* (2012).

She has written in Arabic two books on particular letters of the alphabet: *Hadiyat al-Hamza* (A Present for the Letter Hamza), UAE National Library, 2014, and *Al-Ta' Al-Marbouta Tateer* (The Letter Ta' Escapes), Tamer Institute, Palestine, 2011.

In her introduction to Tasting the Sky, Barakat writes: "To learn about the Middle East, and to deepen our understanding of both Palestinians and Israelis, it helps to share stories. Mine is one of many . . . Together, these stories may inspire us to join hearts and minds so that, with our collective wisdom, a solution for this conflict – and any other – is possible."

Update by Laura Ferreri on

Embrace on Brooklyn Bridge by Ezzedine C Fishere

Ezzedine Fishere's novel *Embrace on Brooklyn Bridge*, now available from Hoopoe Fiction in English translation by John Peate, is an interesting and enjoyable novel that opens a window onto the immigrant's mind and allows the readers to rethink their own society through the eyes of people who do not belong to it.

The original Arabic novel was first published in 2011, and was shortlisted for the 2012 International Prize for Arabic fiction.

A review by Sally Gomaa of this Arabic edition was published in *Banipal 44 – 12 Women Writers* (Summer 2012), and that can be read online at http://www.banipal.co.uk/book_reviews/91/embrace-on-brooklyn-bridge/

The novel shows how difficult it is to explain what it means to be an immigrant. It is not just a choice to move to a country where you believe you will have a better life; it is not about despising your own country and idealizing another one. It is difficult to put into words what an immigrant feels every day towards both their native land and their new home, but Ezzedine Fishere succeeds in putting all of this and more into words in *Embrace on Brooklyn Bridge*, telling the story of eight different characters who are connected to each other because they are friends or relatives of Prof Darwish and his granddaughter Salma, the protagonists of the first and last chapters.

Darwish is an Egyptian professor who has recently been diagnosed with cancer. Having decided to live the rest of his days in a cabin surrounded by nature, he organizes a birthday dinner for Salma, who is visiting from Egypt. The dinner is a chance for Darwish to say goodbye to his friends and family, and organizing it brings to his mind memories of his past. Looking back at major events in his life it becomes clear that his rejection of the Arab world has played an im-

Ezzedine Choukri Fishere

portant role in damaging his relationship with his family.

Most of the stories show how difficult it has been for this group of immigrants to integrate into American society, which is depicted as much more discriminating than what we would like to believe. For example, Adnan, a distant relative of the professor, goes back to visit the neighbourhood of Washington DC where he grew up, and for the first time realizes that the reason behind the existence of two schools in his district is to separate white children from children of colour.

Racial prejudices are also behind the reason why Rabab, a former student of Darwish and close friend of Salma's mother, was fired from a law firm. Clients refused to hire her as their lawyer because of her Arab origin. As a reaction to this event, Rabab decided to focus her career on defending minorities' rights.

Daoud, Darwish's brother-in-law, describes the relationship between the East and the West as the one between David and Goliath. It is a never-ending battle where every action of one party causes a stronger reaction from the other party. In Daoud's view, the bridges that have brought the East and the West close to each other have only allowed them to engage "in a deadly embrace that makes us both suffer".

Embrace on Brooklyn Bridge is translated by John Peate and published by Hoopoe Fiction, Cairo, 1 April 2017. ISBN: 978-977-416-819-2. Pbk, 162pp, US$14.95 / £9.99 / LE180.

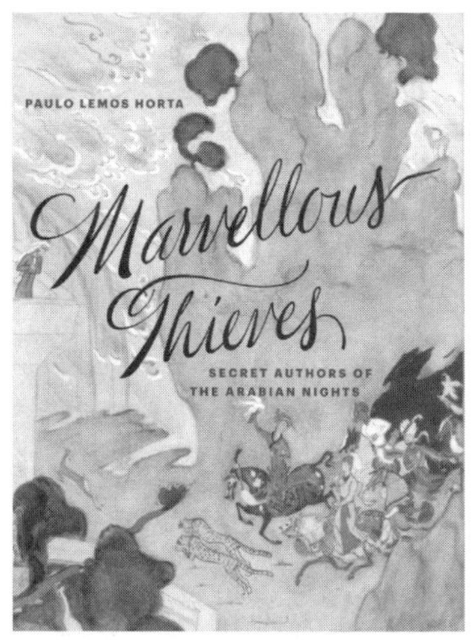

Marvellous Thieves – Secret Authors of the Arabian Nights by Paolo Lemos Horta, is a dogged and dramatic investigation into the sources of the classic French and English translations of the Arabian Nights of the 18th and 19th centuries. Like a detective, Horta uncovers an astounding trail of plagiarisms, inventions and third-hand translations, that becomes a spellbinding story in itself. Harvard University Press, January 2017. ISBN 9780674545052, Hbk, 384pp. $29.95 / £23.95 / €27.00

Maryam: Keeper of Stories by Lebanese author Alawiya Sobh is focused on the time before and during the Lebanese Civil War and depicts the lives and relationships of three women, Alawiyya (the author who is trying to write a novel), Maryam and Ibtisam. Maryam is tasked with holding on to their memories and stories, but refuses to be just a receptacle and tells her own stories. The Arabic original *Maryam al-Hakaya* (Dar al-Adab, 2002), was acclaimed in the Arab world "as a novel of epic dimensions, and provoked numerous articles by literary critics and writers". In 2006 Sobh was awarded the Sultan Qaboos prize for this novel. There are already French, German and Italian editions and now, at last, an English-language one. An earlier version of Chapter 1, also by translator Nirvana Tanoukhi, was published in *Banipal No 17* (Summer 2003). Published by Seagull Books, June 2016. ISBN: 9780857423252. Hbk, 266pp. USD27.50, £20.50.

Zainab by Mohammed Hussein Heikal is lauded as the first modern Egyptian novel written in native vernacular. Originally published in 1913, and adapted for a film of the same name in 1925. Translated by John Mohammed Grinsted. Republished by Darf Publishing, 2017. ISBN 978-1850772903, pbk, 208pp, £8.99.

The Open Door by Latifa Al-Zayyat (1923-1996), translated by Marilyn Booth. A semi-autobiographical novel set during violent demonstrations against the British in Cairo's Tahrir Square in 1946 and the coming to power of Gamal Abdul Nasser, centres around a young Egyptian woman, Layla, growing up striving for personal and political freedom against the familial and societal restrictions of the time. It was originally published in 1960, and was awarded the first Naguib Mahfouz Medal for Literature posthumously in 1996. Al-Zayyat became a professor of English at Ain Shams University in Cairo and presented a model for modern womanhood to many during the 1950s and 1960s. First published in English translation by Marilyn Booth in 2001. Republished by Hoopoe Fiction May 2017. ISBN: 9789774168277. Pbk, USD17.95 / £9.99 / LE180.

No Road to Paradise by Hassan Daoud is the author's tenth novel. Its Arabic original La Tareeq ila al-Janna won the 2015 Naguib Mahfouz Medal for Literature. The setting is a small rural Lebanese village and the protagonist a man suffering from terminal cancer who struggles to make peace with himself, being profoundly dissatisfied with his lot in the world, and questioning traditional life and religion. Translated by Marilyn Booth, who has translated a number of contemporary Arab authors, and is professor of Arabic and the study of the contemporary Arab world at the University of Oxford. Hoopoe Fiction, 1 April 2017. ISBN 9789774168178. Pbk, 304pp, US$17.95 / £11.99 / LE220.

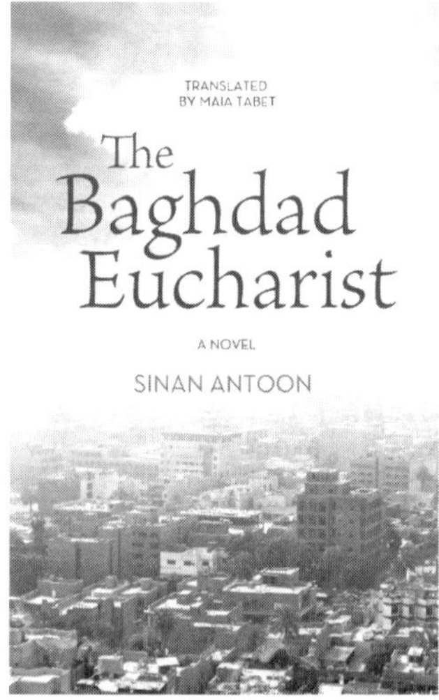

The Baghdad Eucharist by Iraqi author,

poet and academic Sinan Antoon, takes the reader into the lives and experiences of Christian Baghdadis over 24 hours of sectarian attacks and killings, through the eyes of the elderly Youssef and the young woman Maha. Its Arabic original *Ya Mariam* (2012, Manshurat al-Jamal) was shortlisted for the 2013 International Prize for Arabic Fiction, and has an edition in Spanish *Fragmentos de Bagdad* (2014). Translated by Maia Tabet, who has translated many contemporary Arab authors. Hoopoe Fiction, 1 April 2017. ISBN: 9789774168208. Pbk, 130pp. US$14.95 / £9.99 / LE180.

Menorahs and Minarets by Egyptian writer Kamal Rahayyim follows Galal back to Cairo from Paris after ten years. This is the final part of the author's trilogy about the mixed Jewish-Muslim family. Galal is trying to find peace in a life in Cairo, but restrictive conventions of the older generation and his mother continually intervene and he ends up like a lost soul. The other two volumes are available in English translation – *Diary of a Jewish Muslim* (2014) and *Days of Diaspora* (2012), also translated by Sarah Enany. Entered for the 2017 Saif Ghobash Banipal Prize for Arabic Literary Translation. Translated by Sarah Enany. Hoopoe Fiction, March 1st 2017. ISBN: 9789774168314. Pbk, 264pp, US$16.95 / £9.99 / LE180.

The Book of Safety by Yasser Abdel Hafez, an Egyptian journalist and writer based in Cairo, is an intriguing dystopian novel centred on the art of thievery. It opens with protagonist Khaled Mamoun answering an advertisement and finding himself chosen to transcribe testimonies or confessions that are pouring into Cairo's mysterious Palace of Confessions. He becomes enthralled and obsessed by one of his confessors, a professor who doubles as a master thief, and who has written a book about his "profession". Entered for the 2017 Saif Ghobash Banipal Prize for Arabic Literary Translation. Translated by Robin Moger. Hoopoe Fiction, February 2017. ISBN 9789774168215. Pbk, 288 pp. US$16.95 / £9.99 / LE180.

The Queue by Basma Abdel Aziz, longlisted for the 2017 US Best Translated Book Award, is a darkly dystopian novel, surreally modelled on present-day Cairo, but set in a future Arab city ruled by a faceless Big Brother entity called the "Gate" whose authority provoked protests known only as the "Disgraceful Events". Every aspect of daily life requires a stamp of authorization by the "Gate" and a long, winding queue develops which includes the wounded protagonist Yehya who needs authorization to have the bullet removed that lodged in his pelvis during the "events" as all bullets belong to the "Gate". The author is an Egyptian psychiatrist, artist, journalist and well-known campaigner against injustice and repression in Egypt. Translated by Elisabeth Jaquette. Melville House, UK/USA. ISBN 9781612195162. Pbk, 224pp. USD12.76 / £10.68, e-version USD10.99,

Don't Panic, I'm Islamic – Words and Pictures on How to Stop Worrying and Learn to Love the Alien Next Door is a brilliantly bold comedic and satirical response to the US travel ban and includes cartoons, graffiti, photography, colouring in pages, memoir, short stories and more by 34 contributors from around the world, among them Hassan Abdulrazzak, Leila Aboulela, Carol Ann Duffy, Moris Farhi, Alberto Manguel and Laila Shawa. ISBN 9780863569999. 192pp, £12.99 / USD18.95. Edited by Lynn Gaspard, Saqi Books, July 2017.

Tiger and Clay, Syria Fragments by Rana Abdul Fattah is a collection of poems, recollections and comments on the war in Syria, while living in Istanbul and being homesick for Damascus. The author is a Syrian from Damascus, who studied English literature there and in the USA, and went to Istanbul to continue her studies, and then finding herself stuck there by the advent of war. Palewell Press, UK. ISBN 978-0-995535121, pbk, 85pp, £8.99.

Poets and the Algerian War, a bilingual French and English volume, edited by Francis Combes and translated by Alan Dent, features "French poets against the war" including Louis Aragon, Jacques Gaucheron, Madeleine Riffaud, Pierre Seghers and Henri Deluy; "a homage to Maurice Audin", a young university teacher in Algiers who was arrested by French paratroopers, tortured and murdered and "Algerian Poets and the war of liberation" with works by Algerian poets including Jean Sénac, Kateb Yacine, Bachir Hadj Ali, Noureddine Aba, Messaour Boulanouar, Mohammed Dib, Nourredine Tidafi, Malik Haddad and others. Smokestack Books, UK. ISBN: 9780995563537. Pbk, 194pp. £7.99. www.smokestack-books.co.uk

Describing the Past by Ghassan Zaqtan is a half memoir half coming-of-age novella of 17 mini-narratives that dip intriguingly and lovingly into moments of daily life that highlight the family's migration from place to place. Published in Arabic in 1995, and only last year published in English, possibly after Zaqtan's work gained prominence following his poetry collection in English translation by Fady Joudah, *Like a Straw Bird if Follows Me*, winning the 2013 Griffin Poetry Prize. Elegantly translated by Samuel Wilder. Seagull Books, London, NY, Calcutta, July 2016. ISBN: 97808574223498, Hbk, 84pp, USD19 / £11.01. www.seagullbooks.org

Gilgamesh's Snake and Other Poems by Iraqi poet Ghareeb Iskander, and translated by the author with the Scottish poet John Glenday, was awarded the King Fahd Arabic Translation manuscript prize. Published in a bilingual collection by Syracuse University Press (Middle East Literature in Translation), April 2016. ISBN: 978-0815610717, Pbk, 144pp, USD14.95 / £14.95.

Rock in a Hard Place – Music and Mayhem in the Middle East by journalist and heavy metal oficionado Orlando Crowcroft is a fascinating investigatory journey into the heavy metal music scene of Lebanon, Iran, Egypt, Saudi Arabia, Palestine and Israel, and Syria. Crowcroft writes warmly about the many musicians he got to know during his six years' travelling in the region. He records the myriad of players and fans resolutely opposed to extremism, war and ISIS, showing the power of music to bring human beings together across countries and divides – as in the 30,000 fans in Abu Dhabi in 2011 who welcomed Metallica's first ME gig. Published by Zed Books, London. zedbooks.net ISBN: 9781786990150. Pbk, 292pp, £12.99 / US$16.95. Also hb, pdf, epub and mobi editions available.

Kawoosh's *Women of Turquoise*

In April this year, the Iraqi artist Sattar Kawoosh was in London at the Baker Street Alef Bookstore for the launch of his wonderful bilingual Dutch and English collection of artwork, *Vrouwen van Turquoise / Women of Turquoise*. The large-format hardback celebrates Kawoosh's 15 years living as an artist in the Netherlands, and includes 140 pages of paintings, portraits and illustrations. The audience listened enthusiastically as Kawoosh described his journey into being an artist; how as a young boy, he was entranced by patterns of light and how new colours were created out of mixing; and how when he was 12 years old he spent all his pocket money on a book about Rembrandt. Seeing the "Night Watch" for real years later in Amsterdam brought tears to his eyes.

Sattar Kawoosh, born in 1963, won a coveted place to Baghdad's Academy of Fine Art, and as early as 1985 began winning awards for his paintings. He arrived in the Netherlands on New Year's Eve, 1999, and became one of the then large community (75-strong) of Iraqi artists who had gravitated to the country.

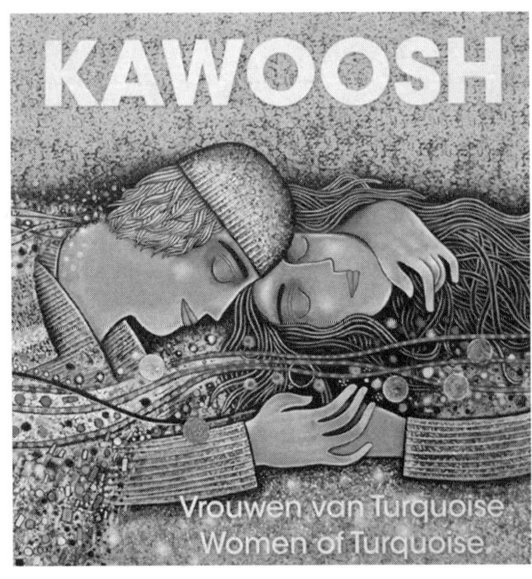

Copies of the book (€ 30.00 plus postage) can be ordered directly from the artist by emailing kawoosh@hotmail.nl. See more at www.kawoosh-art.com

Sattar Kawoosh was the cover artist of *Banipal 45 – Writers from Palestine* (2012), *Banipal 26* (Summer 2006), and created a beautiful Banipal postcard to mark the magazine's 10th anniversary.

A time for literary leaks

Columbia University conference on "Adab as an Interdisciplinary Pursuit"

BEN KOERBER reports

Shortly before giving the Persian spy Barzawayh access to that jealously guarded book of animal fables, *Kalila wa Dimna*, the treasurer of the King of India offers his friend an aphorism: "Preserving secrets is the heart (head) of *adab*". إن حفظ السر رأس الأدب.

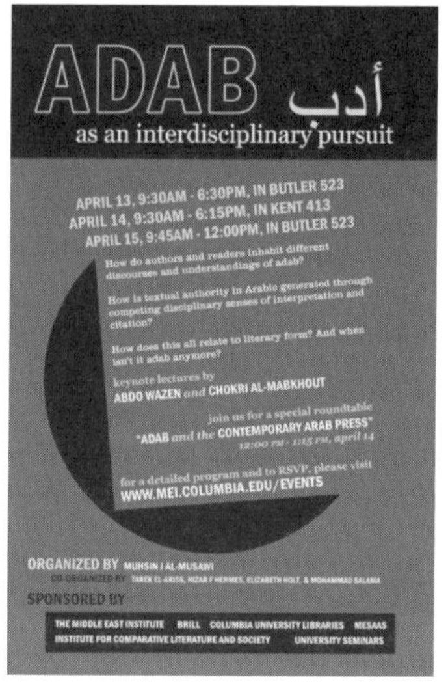

In the context of the story – one of several introductory frames appended by the book's eighth-century Arabic translator, Ibn al-Muqaffa' – the word adab denotes ethics, "honour and integrity" (to borrow Knatchbull's translation). The message seems unambiguous: there is nothing more polite than keeping a friend's secret. In a rigidly hierarchical world, friendship is a matter of confidence secured through the exchange of mutually indemnifying gossip; it is the basis upon which the entire social and political order rests. Yet what follows indicates a paradox. For it turns out that the preservation of the Indians' secret book depends not on its concealment behind lock and key, but on its translation and dissemination to as wide an audience as possible – its leaking, as it were.

An academic conference is a rather exclusive affair, its participants vetted according to the standards, norms, and tastes of the field, and the ideas exchanged therein protected by an implicit vow of confidentiality that lasts until the moment of their publication. We schol-

Columbia University. Photo by Samuel Shimon

ars of the humanities, it must be admitted, guard our research like so many precious secrets. And yet, the ancient wisdom transmitted by Ibn al-Muqaffa' provides sufficient justification for reporting on the issues and intimacies of one such conference, especially as it happens to concern *adab* in all its various shades of meaning. "*Adab* as an Interdisciplinary Pursuit", held at Columbia University, 13–15 April, was the latest conference organized by Professor Muhsin al-Musawi, Professor of Arabic literature and Comparative Cultural Studies at Columbia University, under the aegis of the *Journal of Arabic Literature*, the leading academic journal in its field. The event's title is a clever pun on one of the principle connotations of *adab*: "discipline," especially in the senses of moral as well as physical education, refinement, and control that have so suffused projects and ideologies of modernization, whether in Ibn al-Muqaffa''s time or our own.

Of course, *adab* also means "literature", and this licenses yet another reading of the aphorism uttered above. The preservation – and divulging – of a secret constitutes the "heart (head)" not only of ethics, but of belles lettres. That is to say that this very foundational act of Arabic prose literature – Ibn al-Muqaffa''s *Kalila wa Dimna* – has its origins in a daring feat of espionage, a literary leak.

It was thus appropriate that the conference's first paper, delivered by Tarek El-Ariss, expounded on the "leak" as a metaphor for a pervasive style of authorship in the Arab world and beyond. The author-

Tarek El-Ariss, Mohammed Salama and Anna Ziajka Stanton

cum-leaker, in El-Ariss's formulation, channels not only internationally recognized figures like Julian Assange, Chelsea Manning, and Edward Snowden (and perhaps, more recently, America's deep state whisperers). The concept also links to Arabic writers whose "unruly" speech acts – Twitter spats, blogging confessions, assorted promiscuities of text, technology, and genre – presage not so much the death of the Author as his unwilled suicide through excesses of discourse and divulgence. The broad theoretical appeal of the leak, perhaps, will be found in its ability to banish the postmodernist's favorite bogeyman, the modern liberal subject. In the Arab context, the concept heralds the end of the *nahda*-era ideal of *adab* as refinement, viz. the control of language and affect in the service of the modern repressive apparatus.

(As soon as it was suggested to the conference participants that we "explore the term 'leak' in all its meanings", one could not help but imagine the room's hive mind buzzing with anecdotes about al-Akhtal's famous diatribe against Jarir, and perhaps Ibn Qudama's 12th-century polemic against individuals besieged by demonic whispering or waswasa).

Postmodernism has not been kind to the inherited concepts and categories of literature and society. It is surely a testament to the robustness and efficacy of *adab* that it was able to survive so scandalous a deconstruction as preceded. The remainder of the conference presentations were critical in this regard, as participants rallied to piece

Opening session of the conference

adab back together again, restoring its secrets and reviving its conventional associations to creative ends.

Anna Ziajka Stanton followed with a reading of Aisha Taymur's novel, Consequences of Circumstances in Words and Deeds" (*Nata'ij al-ahwal fi al-aqwal wa al-af'al*, 1886). This tale of scheming ministers, forlorn princes, and "crossings" of gender, genre, geography, and dress – all woven together through saj' or rhymed prose that never skips a beat – has perhaps more in common with *Kalila wa Dimna* than it does with *A Thousand and One Nights*. For Stanton, Taymur's text was an opportunity to revive a notion of *adab* informed by what Aristotle called "ethics": the inculcation of corporeal habits that realize ethical ideals. The result was an understanding of adab that successfully disarmed the term of its associations with didactic violence, while maintaining its potential for ethical and aesthetic transformation.

Both papers served to remind us that although *adab* is at once ethical and literary, it means nothing without a body. The body leaks, the body bleeds; the body speaks, stammers, reels, and resists. The embodied dimensions of *adab* were further developed by Gretchen Head in her presentation on the autobiographical writings of the Moroccan author al-Tuhami al-Wazzani (1903-1972). Combining Sufi models of selfhood with European narrative techniques, al-Wazzani, Head argued, involved readers in an act of anti-colonial resistance

Conference organizer Professor Muhsin al-Musawi with most of the conference participants

Photo by Samuel Shimon

l to r: Shakir Nouri, Abdo Wazin, Samuel Shimon and Tarek El-Ariss

that was both textual and corporeal. Samer Ali's exploration of "scapegoating" in the poetic performances of al-Mutanabbi theorized a literary alternative to a sordid history of bodies scarred, sacrificed, or expelled in the service of social and political harmony. In a thoroughly pedagogical presentation, Nizar Hermes drew our attention to the unjustifiable absence of Arabic humor in college curricula, and the need to more fully incorporate the body that laughs. Yet despite these valuable takes on the embodied dimensions of *adab*, a notable absence during the conference was any significant elaboration on the term's affinities with the alimentary, for example the *ma'duba* or banquet and its etiquette, the arts of avarice and parasitism, perceptions of the raw and the cooked, taste and disgust as civilizational boundary markers – the who-eats-what and the who-eats-who of *Kalila wa Dimna*.

This brings us to politics, which featured in quite a number of papers beyond those mentioned above. Elizabeth Holt examined the weaponization of Arabic literature as an extension of Western imperialist designs, such as the CIA's Congress of Cultural Freedom and its support for the Beiruti journal *al-Hiwar*. Suzanne Stetkevych investigated 13th-century variations on a *khabar* concerning excavations at the Great Mosque of Damascus, suggesting that changes to the historical account could be explained as, among other things, acts of political or ideological propaganda. Teresa Pepe traced the shifting contours of the *adeeb* ("writer/intellectual") in modern Egypt, placing the figure at the intersection of competing political, literary, and cultural discourses. The present writer discussed the work of the outsider artist and self-professed Adeeb al-Shabaab ("The Young Men's *Adeeb*") Mahmud 'Abd al-Raziq 'Afifi, and assessed the extent to which the author's social isolation and idiosyncrasies of style challenge, or reinforce, dominant regimes of adab. Though it did not include an explicit mention of politics, nor of the body, Christian Junge's presentation on "enumeration" in the Arabic tradition may be counted as having contributed to our understanding of both. The insistence of al-Shidyaq on lexical lists drawn from Classical Arabic, in Junge's reading, intervened in contemporary debates on the role of language and adab in modernity. Taken further, the political significance of al-Shidyaq's lists may be located in their object-oriented multiplicity, and thus their affinity with the militantly anti-reductionist trends in recent post-human theory. As concerns the corporeal dimension of enumeration, Junge's evocation of the metaphor of "stringed pearls" calls to mind the Qur'an's promise of youthful cup-bearers.

Conference organizers did not deprive us of these delights, as the second day featured a special panel on "*Adab* and the Contemporary Arab Press", that was one of the most successful highlights of the conference, with Abdo Wazen (cultural editor of *al-Hayat*, and the conference's keynote speaker), *Banipal*'s own Samuel Shimon, and the novelist, journalist, and translator Shakir Noori. The three dispensed generously of their cup of *adab*, offering special insights into the challenges and opportunities facing Arabic literature today. As a matter of course, the banquet allowed for the spilling – and thus preservation – of assorted "secrets": the financing for newspapers and journals provided by certain Arab Gulf countries; the intrigue behind Arabic literary prizes; anecdotes about Eugène Ionesco and Gabriel García Márquez; the corners, crenels, trestles, and trapdoors of the cultural field. All was delivered in a clear Arabic, which, with the exception of an eloquent presentation by Boutheina Khaldi, was largely missing from the remainder of the conference's events.

Any solecisms aside, however, "Adab as an Interdisciplinary Pursuit" held true to its promise of mutual and multifaceted edification, companionship, and delight.

BEN KOERBER

The role of translation in the service of Arabic literature

This year, 2017, Banipal is marking its 20th year of publication with a number of special events throughout the year. The first one was at the Abu Dhabi International Book Fair on 30 April – a panel discussion on "The Role of Translation in the Service of Arabic Literature" with guests literary translator Jonathan Wright, Kuwaiti author Saud Alsanousi and Banipal's editor Samuel Shimon, moderated by Egyptian journalist Maysara Salahadin.

Samuel Shimon spoke about the role of Banipal in promoting and publicising Arab literature in English translation, as well as about the relationship between authors and translators. Today, he said, it is easy to read translations of many established and emerging young authors while 20 years ago before the launch of Banipal this was impossible, adding that there was general agreement on this across the field of Arabic literary translation. Jonathan Wright, who won the 2016 Saif Ghobash Banipal Prize for Arabic Literary Translation for his translation of *Saq al-Bamboo* (*The Bamboo Stalk*) by Saud Alsanousi, said that translators often do not have enough time to read as widely as they should in an ideal world and are dependent on institutions such as Banipal, as well as literary critics and the literary prize network, for tips on the books that are likely to be interesting and, importantly, might be attractive to publishers, who risk their money when they publish literature in translation. He said that he personally did not see himself as an arbiter of literary quality in Arabic in the traditional sense and the publishing world and the reading public should be open-minded about all genres of writing in Arabic, many of which remained undeveloped. He said that one of the pleasures of translating literature was meeting the authors and asking difficult questions, which often led to enlightening cross-cultural dialogues, though in the end human beings everywhere have more in common than they have differences. Saud Alsanousi praised the translation and expressed his gratitude, confirming to the audience that Jonathan had sent him many, many questions by email. He was very pleased with the whole process.

The special events continue with a one-day conference on 20 July at the Moussem Assilah in Morocco with Mohammed Ben Aissa, Robert Irwin, Stefan Weidner, Mohammed al-Achaari, Hartmut Fähndrich,

l to r: Jonathan Wright, Saud Alsanousi, Maysara Salahadin, Samuel Shimon

Kaoru Yamamoto, Isabella Camera d'Afflitto, Khaled Mattawa, Jonathan Wright, Fadhil al-Azzawi, Khaled al-Najjar, Sharafdine Majdouline, Latifa Baqa, Ismail Ghazali, Saif Al-Rahbi, Ahmed el-Madini, Samuel Shimon and Margaret Obank.

Following that, at the International Berlin Literature Festival on 8 September, there will be a celebratory evening with Syrian poet Nouri al-Jarrah, Algerian novelist Amin Zaoui, Emirati writer Mariam Al-Saedi, Egyptian poet Emad Fouad and Slovenian poet Veronika Dintinjana (the latter's work appeared in *Banipal 41*, in the magazine's first non-Arab guest literature feature)

On 2 October Banipal's editor Samuel Shimon is invited to speak about Banipal and the translation of Arabic literature at the Istanbul International Poetry Festival. Later, on 13 October, at the Frankfurt Book Fair, there will be a joint Banipal-ICORN event in the Weltempfang discussing the hot topic "Crises – good for creativity? Literary responses to the ongoing crisis in the Arab World" with Libyan poet Ashur Etwebi, Syrian poet Mohamad Alaaedin Abdul Moula and Samuel Shimon, moderated by Peter Ripkin.

l to r: Samuel Shimon, Mohammed Hasan Alwan, Walid Hamarneh, Fleur Montanaro and Paul Blezard

Literary Awards in the Arab World

Banipal's latest event at Waterstones Piccadilly Bookshop in central London on the evening of 27 June, was a panel discussion about 'Literary Awards in the Arab World'. The well-attended event – supported by the International Prize for Arabic Fiction (IPAF) – was the latest in a fruitful series of Arab literary events organised by Banipal at Waterstones' splendid flagship branch.

The Waterstones evening was a tie-in to *Banipal 58 – Arab Literary Awards*. In addition to its multi-author cover feature on literary awards, the issue includes English translations of excerpts from the six novels shortlisted for IPAF 2017.

The special guest at the Banipal evening was Saudi writer Mohammed Hasan Alwan, winner of IPAF 2017 for his novel *Mawt Saghir* (A Small Death). Alwan had flown to London from Toronto, where he now lives. *Mawt Saghir* – Alwan's fifth novel since 2002 – explores the life and thought of the Sufi saint Muhyiddin Ibn 'Arabi (1165–1240 AD).

The audience much appreciated the chance to hear Alwan talk about the experience of being an IPAF winner, and about his writing career and his prizewinning novel. During the evening Alwan read an excerpt from the novel in Arabic, with IPAF administrator Fleur Montanaro reading Paul Starkey's English translation. In addition to the prize money of US$50,000 plus the US$10,000 that goes to each shortlistee, IPAF guarantees translation into English for the winning novel.

The panel was chaired by Banipal trustee and contributor Paul Blezard. Alongside Alwan and Montanaro were Walid Hamarneh of Qatar's Sheikh Hamad Award for Translation and International Understanding (SHATIU), and Banipal editor Samuel Shimon. The lively panel discussion was followed by a question and answer session with the audience.

Shimon recounted his memories of being IPAF's first chairman of judges in 2008. He also told of how Banipal's publisher Margaret Obank and he established the annual £3,000 award Saif Ghobash Prize for Arabic Literary Translation, which celebrated its tenth anniversary last year. More recently he and Banipal had helped found the Al-Multaqa Arabic Short Story Prize, awarded for the first time in 2016. The prize, worth $20,000, plus the $5,000 that is received by each shortlisted author, is sponsored by the American University in Kuwait (AUK) and Al-Multaqa al-Thaqafi (Cultural Circle), founded and run by Kuwaiti writer Taleb Alrefai. As a result of the new prize "young writers in the Arab world started to come back to writing short stories", Shimon said.

Fleur Montanaro explained how the initial idea for IPAF – which celebrates its tenth anniversary this year – came through a meeting of a leading British publisher and an Arab counterpart at the Frankfurt Book Fair. They "deplored the lack of quality Arabic literature in English and other languages, and the idea came for a prize that would reward the best in Arabic literature, and also fund and promote translation".

Walid Hamarneh noted that the Sheikh Hamad Award for Translation and International Understanding (SHIATIU), now in its third year, started as an award of $40,000 shared between four people or institutions. "But we were able very quickly, within two years, to raise the amount to $2 million every year." The deadline for submissions for the current round of the award is 31 August. There are five awards of $200,000 each (including an Achievement Award), and ten of $100,000 each. The qualifying translations this year are into, or from, Arabic and the following languages: English, French, Chinese, Japanese, Malay, Persian and Urdu. Details can be obtained from www.hta.qa/en

SUSANNAH TARBUSH

BANIPAL ALBUM is a new section in the magazine starting with Banipal 59, which will features photographs of authors, translators and publishers.

All photos by Samuel Shimon

Karam Youssef, Publisher, Kotob Khan Publishing, Cairo, Egypt

Hassan Yaghi, Publisher, Dar al-Tanweer, Beirut, Lebanon

Bachar Chebaro, Publisher, Difaf Publishing, Beirut, Lebanon

Assia Mousaoui, Publisher, Ikhtilaf Editions, Algiers, Algeria

Nur al-Huda Mohammad Nur al-Huda, Publisher, Azza Pubishing House, Khartoum, Sudan

Yassin Adnan is a Moroccan writer and broadcaster, born in Safi, Morocco, in 1970. Since his early childhood he has lived in Marrakech and for over 20 years has worked in cultural journalism. In 1991, he published the *Contemporary Voices* magazine and then *Poetry Raid*,which embodied the new poetic sensibility prevalent in Morocco in the early 1990s. Since 2006, he has researched and presented the weekly cultural television programme "Masharif". He is the author of four books of poetry, three short story collections, a book (with Saad Sarhan) about Marrakech, *Marrakech: Open Secrets* (2008) and *The Moroccan Sheherazade: Testimonies and Studies of Fatima Mernissi* (2016). *Hot Maroc* (2016), longlisted for the 2017 IPAF, is his first novel.

Mohammed Hasan Alwan is a Saudi Arabian novelist, born in Riyadh, Saudi Arabia in 1979. He graduated with a doctorate in International Marketing from the University of Carleton, Canada. Alwan has published five novels to date: *The Ceiling of Sufficiency* (2002), *Sophia* (2004), *The Collar of Purity* (2007), *The Beaver* (2011), and *A Small Death* (2016), as well as a non-fiction work, *Migration: Theories and Key Factors* (2014). His work has appeared in translation in *Banipal* magazine (Blonde Grass and Statistics, translated by Ali Azeriah), in *The Guardian* (Oil Field, translated by Peter Clark), and in *Words Without Borders* (Mukhtar, translated by William M. Hutchins). In 2009-10, Alwan was chosen as one of the 39 best Arab authors under the age of 40 by the Beirut39 project and his work was published in the *Beirut39* anthology. He was also a participant in the first IPAF Nadwa in 2009 and a mentor on the Nadwa in 2016. In 2013, *The Beaver* was shortlisted for the International Prize for Arabic Fiction and in 2015, its French edition (translated by Stéphanie Dujols) won the Prix de la Littérature Arabe awarded in Paris for the best Arabic novel translated into French for that year.

Sultan Al Ameemi is an Emirati writer born in Al Dhaid, the UAE, in 1974. He has published 19 books: 14 studies of popular culture in the UAE, three collections of short stories and two novels: *P.O. Box 1003* (2014). and *One Room Is Not Enough* (2016) which was longlisted for the 2017 IPAF. For the past seven seasons, he has been a judge of the AUAE's Million's Poet contest. In 2014, he took part in the IPAF Nadwa for talented young writers , where he began work on *One Room Is Not Enough*. He is currently director of the Abu Dhabi Arabic Poetry Academy and writes a weekly column on cultural matters in the *Al-Emarat Al-Youm* newspaper.

Sinan Antoon is a poet, novelist and translator born in Iraq in 1967. He has published four novels, *I'jaam: An Iraqi Rhapsody* (2004); *The Pomegranate Alone* (2010), published in his own English translation as *The Corpse Washer* in 2013 and awarded the 2014 Saif Ghobash Banipal Prize for Arabic Literary Translation, as well as being longlisted for the Independent Foreign Fiction Prize 2014; *Hail Mary* (2012), shortlisted for the 2013 IPAF and published in Spanish as *Fragmentos de Bagdad* (2014); and *Index* (2016), longlisted for the 2017 IPAF; also a volume of poetry *A Night in Every Town* (2007, published in English as *The Baghdad Blues*). His writings have been translated into eight languages. In 2003, he directed a documentary film in Baghdad called *About Baghdad* (2004), which dealt with Baghdad after dictatorship and occupation. He has translated the poetry of Mahmoud Darwish, Sargon Boulus, Saadi Youssef and others into English. Antoon has taught Arabic literature at the University of New York since 2005.

Laila al-Atrash is a Palestinian/Jordanian novelist, born in Beit Sahour, east of Bethlehem, in 1948. Her novels and short stories have been translated into several languages, including English, French, Italian, Korean, and Hebrew, and have been added to university curriculums in Jordan, France and America. In 2007, she helped to establish the 'Library of the Family' and 'Reading for All' projects in Jordan, and her social and cultural programmes have won numerous prizes at television and radio festivals. In the 2015 Human Development Report, she was among a small number of women writers who were deemed to have been influential in their societies. She has published one short story collection, two plays and nine novels, including: *The Sun Rises in the West* (1998), *Two Nights . . . and the Shadow of A Woman* (1998), *Ports of Delusion* (2006), *Women at the Crossroads* (2009) and *Hymns ofTemptation* (2014) which was longlisted for the 2016 IPAF.

Peter Bush is an award-winning literary translator. His recent translations into English are Joan Sale's *Winds of the Night* and Prudenci Bertrana's *Josafat* from Catalan and Jorge Carrión's *Bookshops* and Carmen Boullosa's *Before* from Spanish. He also translates works from French and Portuguese.

Raphael Cohen is a translator based in Cairo and a contributing editor of *Banipal*. His recent Arabic fiction translations include Mona Prince's *So You May See* (2011) & *Status: Emo* by Eslam Mosbah.

Amir Tag Elsir is a Sudanese novelist and writer who lives and works in Qatar, and has published 16 novels. He has been shortlisted for the 2011 IPAF and longlisted twice, in 2014 and 2017. See pages 30-41 above.

Ibrahim Farghali is an Egyptian writer, born in Mansoura in 1967. He has a BA in Business Studies from Mansoura University and works as a journalist on the staff of *Al-Arabi* magazine in Kuwait. He has previously worked in the UAE and Oman, and for *Al-Ahram* newspaper in Cairo. He has published three short story collections and six novels, including: *The Cave of Butterflies* (1998), *Smiles of Saints* (2004) which was published in English by the American University in Cairo in 2007, *Genie in a Bottle* (2007) and *Sons of Gebalawi* (2009), winner of the 2012 Sawiris Cultural Award. *The Temple of Silken Fingers,* which was longlisted for the 2016 IPAF and also won the 2017 Sawiris Award. His short story "Body Map", translated by Thomas Aplin, was published in *Banipal 49 – A Cornucopia of Short Stories.*

Laura Ferreri has a BA in interpreting and translation (Trieste University, Italy) and an MA in Arabic Translation (Edinburgh Univ. CASAW). She is a regular Banipal reviewer.

Ghenwa Hayek is an Assistant Professor of Arabic at Claremont McKenna College in Claremont, California. She was born in Beirut, Lebanon. She received her PhD in Comparative Literature from Brown University, writing her dissertation on the representation of Beirut in contemporary Lebanese novels.

Samira Kawar is an energy journalist and literary translator. She has contributed translations to *Banipal* since its foundation in 1998, and is a trustee of the Banipal Trust for Arab Literature. Two of her literary translations from Arabic to English have been published – the novel *The Eye of the Mirror* by Palestinian writer Liana Badr, and the autobiography of the late Saudi writer Abdul Rahman Munif *Story of a City: A Childhood in Amman.*

Renée Hayek is a Lebanese novelist, born in southern Lebanon in 1959. She studied Philosophy at the Lebanese University before embarking on a career in journalism, literary translation and teaching. She has published two collections of short stories and eleven novels including: *The Well and the Sky* (1997), *The Land of the Snows* (2001), *Days of Paris* (2004), *Prayer for the Family* (2007) which was longlisted for the 2009 IPAF, *A Short Life* (2010), longlisted for the 2011 IPAF, and *The Year of the Radio* (excerpted above), longlisted for the 2017 IPAF.

Zuheir al-Hiti is an Iraqi writer and journalist, born in 1957 and currently living in Germany. He has published three novels: *My Distant Day* (2002), *American Dust* (2009) and *Days of Dust* (2016), which was longlisted for the 2017 IPAF, as well as an academic study, *The Image of the Iraqi in the Arabic Novel* (2006).

Julia Ihnatowicz was born in London, where she is currently working as a freelance translator of Arabic. She studied literature at Warwick University, prior to living and working in the Middle East over several years. She has subsequently completed an MA in translation at SOAS and worked on projects ranging from the commercial to the creative.

Abdelkarim Jouaiti (Jouaity) was born in Beni Mellal, capital of the Tadla-Azilal province of Morocco, in 1962, and currently is director of the Ministry of Culture for this region. He is the author of seven novels: *Night of the Sun* (1992) winner of the Moroccan Writers' Union Prize for Young Authors, *Pomegranate of the Insane* (1998), *City of Brass* (2004), *Celebrations of Death* (1996), which is also available in French, *Yellow Morella* (2002), *Platoon of Ruin* (2007), longlisted in the 2009 IPAF and The Moroccans (2016), longlisted for the 2017 IPAF. He has also published other books and translations.

Ben Koerber is an assistant professor of Arabic in the Department of African, Middle

Eastern, and South Asian Languages and Literatures at Rutgers University. He is the translator of Ahmed Naji and Ayman Al Zorkany's novel, *Using Life* (Istikhdam al-Haya), forthcoming from the University of Texas Press in 2017.

Becki Maddock is a translator and researcher living in London. She translates from Arabic, Persian and Spanish into English. She has a first class BA in Arabic and Spanish (Exeter University) and an MA in Near and Middle Eastern Studies from SOAS, University of London. She is now taking Kurdish language classes, also at SOAS.

Charis Olszok is a Lecturer in Modern Arabic Literature and Culture, and a Bye-Fellow and Director of Studies for King's College, University of Cambridge. She studied French and Arabic at the University of Oxford, before going on to complete her MA in Arabic Literature and her PhD at SOAS, with a scholarship from the Wolfson Foundation. Her fiction translations include *African Titanics* by Abu Bakr Khaal, *Ebola '76* by Amir Tag Elsir (co-translation with Emily Danby) and forthcoming by Banipal Books, *Goat Mountain* by Habib Selmi.

John Peate studied Arabic in Morocco, Egypt, Syria and Oman as well as in the UK, and has taught Arabic, translation theory and practice and interpreting at the Universities of Salford and Leeds. He is a regular translator for *Banipal*, and has translated other works by a number of contemporary Arab authors, including *Embrace on Brooklyn Bridge* by Ezzedine Fishere, whose Arabic original was shortlisted for the 2012 IPAF.

Nancy Roberts is a well-known translator of contemporary Arabic fiction, with her translations including works by Naguib Mahfouz, Ghada Samman (including her trilogy), Ibrahim Nasrallah (four novels), Ahlam Mostaghanemi (two novels), Hala El-Badry, Ahlam Bsharat, Laila Aljohani and Salwa Bakr.

Habib Selmi is a Tunisian author, settled in France for many years. He has nine novels and two short story collections. He has been shortlisted twice for the International Prize for Arabic Fiction, in 2009 for *The Scents of Marie-Claire*, which was published in English in 2010, and in 2012 with *The Women of Al-Bassatin*. Five of his novels have French editions with Actes Sud, including *Jabal al-Anz (Goat Mountain)*, his debut novel of 1988, excerpted abovel

Mbarek Sryfi is from Morocco and is currently a lecturer in Arabic language at the University of Pennsylvania, where he is also pursuing a PhD in Arabic Literature and Islamic Studies. He has a first degree in English Literature from the University of Sidi Mohammed Ben Abdellah in Fez, Morocco, and an MA from the École Normale Supérieure in Rabat. He has been a visiting professor at Al-Akhawayn University, Ifrane, Morocco.

Susannah Tarbush is a freelance journalist specialising in cultural affairs in the Middle East. She writes the Tanjara blog, and is a consulting editor of *Banipal* and regular reviewer.

Valentina Viene is Italian by birth, now settled in the UK. She has a BA in Arabic and English from the University of Naples L'Orientale, and an MA in the Theory and Practice of Arabic Translation.

Jonathan Wright is a prizewinning translator who worked for many years as a journalist in the Arab world. His translations include three IPAF winners, Ahmed Sadawi's *Frankenstein in Baghdad* (2014), Saud Alsanousi's *The Bamboo Stalk* (IPAF 2013 & 2016 Saif Ghobash Banipal Prize), and Youssef Ziedan's *Azazeel* (IPAF 2009 & 2013 Saif Ghobash Banipal Prize), and Hassan Blasim's *The Iraqi Christ* (2014 Independent Foreign Fiction Prize).

Viktoria Nikolaevna Zarytovskaya (born 1979) holds a PhD in pedagogical sciences, is a Russian arabist, translator of fiction from Arabic to Russian (among the works – novels by Naguib Mahfouz and Alaa Al Aswany), an author of Arabic language manuals for universities and about thirty scientific papers on modern Arabic Literature, Arabic grammar and methods of teaching Arabic. At present she is associate professor of the Russian University of Peoples' Friendship.

For more information on all the authors in *Banipal 59* and all the translators, writers and book reviewers, please go to:
www.banipal.co.uk/contributors/